Christian Experience in Theology and Life

Christian Experience in Theology and Life

*Papers read at the 1984 Conference of the
Fellowship of European Evangelical Theologians*

edited by

I. Howard Marshall
Professor of New Testament Exegesis
University of Aberdeen

RUTHERFORD HOUSE BOOKS
Edinburgh

Published by Rutherford House, 17 Claremont Park,
Edinburgh EH6 7PJ, Scotland

SCOTTISH BULLETIN OF EVANGELICAL THEOLOGY
SPECIAL STUDY 2

ISBN 0 946068 32 1

Copyright © 1988 Rutherford House and Contributors

All rights reserved. No part of this publication may be reproduced, stored in a retrieval system, or transmitted, in any form, by any means, electronic, mechanical, photocopying, recording or otherwise without the prior permission of Rutherford House.

Cover photograph: The mosaic of the cross in the main meeting room of the Neues Leben-Zentrum, Altenkirchen, West Germany. It is reproduced by kind permission of Anton Schulte.

Computer typeset at Rutherford House on Apple Macintosh™
Printed and bound in Singapore by Chong Moh Offset Printing Private Ltd.

Contents

PREFACE I. Howard Marshall	vi
1. Christian Theology in a World Crying out for Experience Derek J. Tidball	1
2. Prophecy and Spiritual Gifts Then and Now Max Turner and David Mackinder	16
3. Luther and the *Schwärmer* David F. Wright	55
4. Christian Experience and Divine Revelation in the Theologies of Friedrich Schleiermacher and Karl Barth Alan J. Torrance	83
5. Experience in Theology since Barth Christina Baxter	114
6. The Experience of Conversion Helmut Burkhardt	139
7. The Experience of Guidance by the Holy Spirit Siegfried Liebschner	159
8. Towards a Biblical Theology of Experience Klaas Runia	175

PREFACE

Every two years the Fellowship of European Evangelical Theologians (FEET) meets to discuss some theological topic of contemporary significance. At its meeting at the Neues Leben Zentrum, Altenkirchen, W. Germany, in August, 1984, the topic was 'Christian Experience in Theology and Life'. Main papers were given on different aspects of the theme in plenary sessions, and these were complemented by workshop discussions on more specialised areas. Each day's proceedings included times for Bible study and prayer at which expositions of appropriate biblical passages (not included here) were given.

Three reasons determined the choice of the topic. First, there was the consciousness that we are living in an era in which people are craving for experiences of various kinds, seen at its most extreme form in the desire for drug-induced hallucinations. Second, there is the new emphasis on the place of experience in the Christian life both individual and corporate, which finds expression in what is broadly called the 'charismatic' movement. Third, there is the continuing debate in the history of theology over the relative places of objective revelation and subjective religious experience in the apprehension of God and his Word.

These concerns are directly reflected in the contents of the conference addresses and working papers which are offered in this volume.

The setting in the contemporary world, within which and in relation to which the theologian must carry on his task, is sketched for us by Dr Derek J. Tidball, formerly Director of Studies at London Bible College and now minister of Mutley Baptist Church, Plymouth. Dr Tidball is the author of An *Introduction to the Sociology of the New Testament* (Paternoster Press) and an introduction to pastoral theology, *Skilful*

Shepherds (Inter-Varsity Press).

The place of spiritual gifts in the early church and today was the subject of a lengthy paper by Dr Max Turner. Unfortunately it was too detailed to be included in its original form here, and we are grateful for the co-operation of Mr David Mackinder in preparing a shorter version for this volume. The full form is available in *Vox Evangelica* 15, 1985, 7-64. Dr Turner is Lecturer in New Testament at London Bible College, and is currently 'on loan' as a Teaching Fellow in the Department of New Testament, University of Aberdeen.

Three main areas of historical theology are discussed next. Mr David F. Wright, Senior Lecturer in Ecclesiastical History in the University of Edinburgh, takes us into the area of Reformation controversies with his discussion of Luther's relationships with the so-called 'enthusiasts'.

Professor Alan J. Torrance of Knox College, Dunedin, New Zealand, is our guide to the two 'giants' of modern theology, Friedrich Schleiermacher and Karl Barth, in whose thinking 'experience' played a notable part.

The most recent era of theological thought is surveyed by Dr Christina Baxter, Registrar at St John's College, Nottingham.

Two essays look at the area of practical Christian living and the place of experience in it. Dozent Pfr Helmut Burkhardt, who teaches at St Chrischona Theological Seminary, discusses the experience of conversion. He is already known to English readers for his booklet on the closely related topic, *The Biblical Doctrine of Regeneration* (Paternoster Press).

Dozent P. Siegfried Liebschner offers a study of the problems of guidance by the Holy Spirit. He is a lecturer at the Evangelical Free Church Theological Seminary in Hamburg.

Both of these essays have appeared in their original German forms in the *Jahrbuch für evangelikale Theologie 1987* (R. Brockhaus Verlag); we are grateful to Revd David Couper and Miss Morag Marshall respectively for the English translations.

Finally, Professor Klaas Runia, who teaches practical theology at the Reformed Theological Seminary, Kampen, Netherlands, and who is currently the Chairman of the Fellowship of European Evangelical Theologians, draws the threads of the discussion together with some suggestions for a biblical theology of experience.

The editor and contributors are grateful for this opportunity of presenting their thoughts to a wider public in this special study of *The Scottish Bulletin of Evangelical Theology*; our thanks are especially due to Dr Nigel Cameron, the editor of the Bulletin, and to the staff of Rutherford House, who have undertaken much of the task of production.

I. Howard Marshall

CHRISTIAN THEOLOGY IN A WORLD CRYING OUT FOR EXPERIENCE

DEREK J. TIDBALL

Even the most cautious observer would argue that the Western World has undergone a fundamental change in culture since the 1960s. The change is not as radical or complete as its proponents hoped nor as its opponents feared. Nonetheless, it is unmistakable and real. It is a shift which has brought the quest for 'experience' to the centre of the stage. Whatever else the complex word 'experience' may mean,[1] its root means 'to explore by travelling' or 'to acquire experimentally'. In comparison with recent centuries the latter half of the twentieth century has emphasised the desire and right of man to experience for himself, that is to receive knowledge through direct sensory perception, through feeling, and has even encouraged his right to ecstasy. It is on this basis, rather than on the basis of received traditions and wisdom, of reason or of objective facts,[2] that perceptions are formed and interpretations of life are founded. 'I know' or 'I think' has been replaced by 'I feel'. The objective has had to make way for the subjective and man has become preoccupied with the inward quest for self-fulfillment.

A Theoretical Framework

Peter Berger, with other sociologists of knowledge, argues that man is a creative being who constructs his own meaning of life and interpretation of reality and holds on to it in the face of the threat of chaos and irrealities. Each of us encounters marginal experiences, such as dreams, death, madness and ecstasy, which threaten to undermine

1. See Dietmar Mieth, 'What is Experience?' *Concilium* 113, 1979, pp. 40-53.
2. R. D. Laing, *The Voice of Experience*, Harmondsworth, 1983, pp. 9-14. Laing strongly contrasts experience and objective facts.

the order of the normal world we have socially defined.[3] For the most part we stave off the chaos by creating a world of order where everything knows its place. But for a variety of reasons the neat order of yesteryear is no longer adequate to cope with the world of today. Capitalism generated an ideology which was rational, calculative, efficient and instrumental and which left little room for the expressive aspects of life which were exiled from the public into the private sphere.[4] There, aided by the philosophic seeds sown by existentialism, it was able to give full flower to the thrust of Romanticism. Elements, therefore, which had threatened chaos and irreality previously, now became the object of fascination and the subject of experience. In the expressive sphere people desired to tread, the path of a mystical ascent to infinity or of descent into the abyss.

Many would see the work of Victor Turner, an anthropologist, as providing us with the best framework for interpreting that change.[5] Turner's study of *The Ritual Process*[6] led him to posit that all ritual involved an ideological (moral) and a sensory (experiential) dimension. Dynamic rituals, such as a rite of passage, where a movement from one role to another was involved, also involved a stage of liminality. Liminality is a transition stage when one occupies no man's land and where neither the social identity one has just left nor to which one is moving fits. Liminality, in pure form, only lasts for a brief period but it involves the breaking of taboos and a freedom of experimentation which would be normally unacceptable. It is characterized by two features; the creation of anti-structure and of communitas. Anti-structure attacks the boundaries, limits, certainties, conventions, taboos, roles and structures of accepted life.

3. P. L. Berger, *The Social Reality of Religion,* Harmondsworth, 1973, p. 33.
4. D. Bell, *The Cultural Contradictions of Capitalism*, London, 1976.
5. B. Martin, *A Sociology of Contemporary Cultural Change*, Oxford, 1981, p. 49.
6. Ithaca, 1977.

Communitas is the spontaneous creation of pure unmediated sacred community where normal structures no longer apply and social ecstasy is reached.[7] The rejection of society's institutions, conventions and roles causes the participants in a liminal period to look for fulfillment through subjective feelings and many of the features of liminality, as Turner describes them, relates closely to man's present search for experience.

Turner argues that what happens within the microcosm of an initiation rite serves as a model for wider patterns within society and that there many seek to hold on to the creation of spontaneous communitas and translate it into normative communitas. Not only is this to be seen in the recurring patterns of millennarian movements or of radical Christian groups but it is also evidenced within the developments of whole cultures. It is just such a transition or liminal period that Western Europe has been experiencing in recent decades that has given rise to the rejection of normative structures and controls and the growth of anti-structure and communitas with its consequent emphasis on the search for experience. No longer are people content to fulfil an assigned social role in an ordered and structured world. Even where they continue to do so, on the one hand, in the public world of work, on the other hand, in the private world of leisure, they allow the quest of self-fulfillment to take precedence.

A Cursory Survey

Illustrations of the rejection of structure and the search for reality in experience abound in the Western world and symptoms of it are evident in Eastern Europe. The sixties made more available on a mass level trends which had been long established in art. The art of the sixties drew on the movement associated with Dada which embraced meaninglessness and incomprehensibility. Surrealism had already given expression to the subconscious, the irra-

---

7. Ibid., pp. 94 – 130

tional had made poetry of the absurd. Expressionism had introduced a style which expressed the feel and the spiritual values of its subject matter. After the sixties these and even wider trends were drawn upon to break all conventions and taboos. Pictures were not framed, were not classical representations, overrode distinctions between decent and indecent, sacred and profane, good taste and bad, sense and nonsense, the humane and the cruel and even the artist and the observer. Today, as Michael Compton, the organiser of the Exhibition New Art at the Tate, put it, 'artists use anything that comes to hand but underlying that, the values normally given to free and empathetic paintwork are found in many new works. They are: strength of feeling, energy, freedom, a defiance of intellectualism and so on'.[8]

The same trends of anti-structure are found in films, the theatre and literature. A recent review of films spoke of the way in which they give clues as to how one might be able 'to lead a full and authentic emotional life, in the equally full awareness of the virtual all-pervasiveness of emotional manipulation.'[9] The films featured included *Jubilee* made in the year of Queen Elizabeth II's Silver Jubilee which was also the year of the Punk, and portrayed 'a quasi-mystical allegory of English history in which the first Queen Elizabeth travels forward in time to an uncertain date when her erstwhile realm travels forward to the anarchic shambles of Punk apocalyptic vision'.[10] They also featured Andy Warhol who again overrides all conventional structures. Many of his films have no narrative or time sequence. They concern trivia such as *Eat*, *Haircut*, and *Sleep*, which depict their titles. They leave sexual identities uncertain. And they use ordinary people to play themselves rather than actors. There are more main-line

8. Cited in the 'New Art at the Tate', *Art Monthly*, October, 1983, p. 18. For a review of the whole area see H. Rookmaaker, *Modern Art and the Death of Culture*, London, 1970.
9. G. Watson, *New Art Audio Visual*, London, 1983, p. 10.
10. *Ibid.*, p. 11.

films such as *Ordinary People* or *Kramer versus Kramer* which are intensely introverted and show the quest for experience in different ways. Some films, such as *Chariots of Fire*, still represent the world of order and structure and stand as a contrast to the more common anti-structure of the film world. In music the ultimate expression of this was seen not in the random music, such as that of Stockhausen, that broke every rule of tone, harmony, key and melody but in John Cage's *Four Minutes Thirty Three Seconds*, where the performer sits for exactly that time in front of a closed piano before leaving the stage. The purpose of this is to find authentic experience, for 'inside silence we are wholly free, everything is equally significant and man is joined to over arching infinity'.[11]

While the zenith of the search for experience is found in ecstasy through the use of drugs and the resort to sex, it is elsewhere that most people are affected. The primary carriers of these cultural changes are not to be found in elite art but in pop culture, education and the media. It is difficult to appreciate now how revolutionary were the rock n' roll musicians of the 50s and the Beatles with their short hair and ties! But they were revolutionary in their day and unleashed a whole range of styles which again rode roughshod over accepted standards and taboos in a search for authenticity. That search led equally to the protest songs of Dylan and the aggressive destructiveness of Alice Cooper. There is little new on the current scene but the defiance of normal structure continues. The top of the pop charts throughout this year in the UK have been dominated by Frankie Goes to Hollywood and his record 'Relax' which is an explicit manifesto for Gay Sex and 'Two Tribes' which is an anti-war rhetoric whose accompanying video parodies Reagan and Chernenko. Boy George and Divine would be other perfect illustrations of the desire to break free from sexual constraints in order to discover freedom.

11. B. Martin, *op.cit.*, p. 107.

When a historian of Rock can say that its supreme aesthetic achievement is reached when it 'speaks in an unknown tongue' and expresses the inexpressible, the experiential dimension and religious nature of rock becomes clear.[12]

In education the changes have been vast. The student protest movements which reached their peak in 1968 have led to lasting changes in education which have again set out to obscure boundaries and create meaning. The Plowden Report set out the ideal as allowing children to be themselves and to develop in a way and at a pace appropriate to them. Rules of grammar were therefore abandoned; pupil power was recognised; the disciplinary authority of teachers reduced and examinations invented for which there was no passmark.

All this filters down to the masses most of all through the media. Those who have never heard of surrealism may still enjoy the popular shows such as 'Monty Python's Flying Circus' or 'The Rocky Horror Show'. Those who do not take seriously the philosophy of hard rock still imbibe its ethos through radio chat shows.

It is here that the changes can be most exactly documented not least as in England they are epitomized in one man. Hugh Carlton Greene became Director-General of the BBC in 1959 and soon introduced revolutionary changes. He was an agnostic, committed not to upholding moral standards but to 'telling it like it is'. He refused to be the servant of anyone – church, government or establishment – and was going to explore issues hidden before and to enjoy 'frightening the pants off the establishment'.[13] Nothing was sacred except for the commitment to discover illusive truth. Soon new forms of drama and entertainment were introduced, satire was receiving top ratings and sex and bad language were becoming more and more explicit.

12. R. Meltzer, *The Aesthetics of Rock*, Millerton, 1970, pp. 112f.
13. M. Tracey, *A Variety of Lives. A Biography of Sir Hugh Greene*, London, 1983, p. 181.

Greene's story is the personification of contemporary culture and it reads pathetically. The search for freedom and experience had never been so unfettered but it ended in pathetic disappointment. His biographer speaks of him now as a sad and lonely old man who for a brief moment found his ideal love only to let it slip away again never more to fill his emotional vacuum.[14]

Two other areas bring the experiential dimension of the current period of liminality into even sharper focus. They are firstly the trends in psychology and secondly the efflorescence of new religious movements. In his review of contemporary psychology Paul Vitz has shown how egotistical it is. Studying Fromm, Carl Rogers, Abraham Maslow and Rollo May and the more popular movements they have spawned, again and again it is the fully experiencing self which they are concerned with. For Rogers the fifth stage, and therefore an advanced stage of his therapy, is aimed at fully experiencing feelings and to allow them to 'bubble through in spite of fear and mistrust so that they can be experienced with fulness and immediacy'.[15] Maslow believes the ideal person is one who is self-actualized which means, among other things that he will have 'peak' experiences which can be described as oceanic or mystic. Rollo May's is a thoroughly existential psychology which seeks to lead to an intense fundamental awareness of one's existence where the distinction between the experiencing subject and the experienced object is rejected.

Popularly the same trends are manifest in Encounter Groups to which three-quarters of a million people belonged in 1970; in EST, which training encourages people to let go of the notions they were told about and to become fully alive to themselves and in self-help sexual therapies and ideas of open marriage. Often such therapies are not dealing with psychological problems so much as providing

---
14. *Ibid.*, pp. 317f.
15. P. Vitz, *Psychology as Religion*, Grand Rapids, 1977, p. 22.

people with a crumb of stimulation in the midst of a famine caused by boredom.

The actual resort to these psychological therapies is only the tip of the iceberg. They are the extreme expression of a general world view as Daniel Yankelovich's carefully researched *New Rules* shows. The ideas of the avante-garde of the 1960s are now, he argues, much more generally accepted even though it is only a hard-core of 17% of the population which would exhibit it in a strong form. Millions of Americans, however, would to a lesser degree base their lives on the principle' I have a duty to myself' and 'I must be true to my real self'. For the first time in history, he suggests, assigned social roles are being rejected and duty and self-denial are being replaced by a refusal to deny oneself anything and the idea that the inner and presumably more real self must be the arbiter of life.[16]

The same quest for the true self is to be seen in the explosion of New Religious Movements. Here, whilst traditional religious groups which have epitomised the rationalism of their age have been on the decline, the most absurd and culturally displaced religions which offer antistructure and communitas have been able to flourish. As Robert Bellah has commented, 'the catholic church finally decided to recognise the value of the modern world just when American youth were beginning to find it valueless'.[17] The sixties and seventies has been a time of marked spiritual ferment. It has been estimated that 5 per cent of the 21-35 age group in the USA have had exposure to a New Religious Movement of an oriental kind.[18] Few

16. D. Yankelovich, *New Rules Searching for Self-Fulfillment in a World Turned Upside Down*, New York, 1981, pp. xviii and 69.
17. R. N. Bellah, 'New Religious Consciousness and the Crisis of Modernity', C. Glock and R. Bellah (eds.), *The New Religious Consciousness*, London, 1976, pp. 333-352.
18. Although it is difficult to analyse the plethora of New Religious Movements they fall into three categories: neo-orthodoxy,

would dissent[19] from the conclusion that one of the major features of these New Religious Movements is that they offer the possibility of intense emotional commitment, usually although not always in a strong community, and provide for intense subjective experience.[20] As Joseph Fitcher has put it, when we cut through the undergrowth such movements have to do with 'an encounter with truth, transcendence, the sacred'.[21] Erica Heftmann in her personal account of being entrapped by the Moonies describes the climax of her own experience when she had been to a great rally at Yankee Stadium with Moon in these words 'It mattered little where I would go or what I would do. The core of my being was emblazoned, sealed with the destiny of mankind. I was one with the Father.'[22] Others would use different terminology and describe a different event but all would be talking fundamentally about a similar intense spiritual experience. It is interesting to note, by the way, that because of this the converted adolescent evangelical is least likely to be a convert to a New Religious Movement. They have already had their experience and defined their boundaries and found their meanings. It is where these are lacking that a person becomes a potential convert.[23]

---

   counter-cultural or neo-oriental and human potential movements.
19. One who offers an alternative explanation is C. Campbell in 'Some Comments on the New Religious Movements. The New Spirituality and Post-Industrial Society', E. Barker (ed.), *New Religious Movements, A Perspective for Understanding Society*, New York, 1982, pp. 232-242.
20. See, for example, J. D. Hunter, 'The New Religions: Demodernization and the Protest Against Modernity', pp. 1-19, and D. Martin, 'Disorientations in New Religious Movements', pp. 43-58, in B. Wilson (ed.), *The Social Impact of New Religious Movements*, New York, 1981.
21. J. Fitcher, 'Youth in Search of the Sacred', *ibid.*, p. 35.
22. E. Heftmann, *Dark Side of the Moonies*, Harmondsworth, 1983, p. 186.
23. D. Martin, *op. cit.*, p. 56.

It cannot be accidental that at the same time as society generally has been in search of experience and at the same time as there has been the growth of New Religious Movements which emphasised spiritual experience, orthodox Christianity has witnessed the growth of Charismatic renewal. Charismatic renewal began amongst an elite in the early 1960s and it was not until the 1970s that some of its tenants were accepted by mainline churches, and perhaps too diluted by them, and that new movements wholly committed to renewal broke away from mainline churches. The complexity of the charismatic movement means that charismatics are best identified by their homogeneity of experience. Their freedom in the expression of worship; an anti-structure which often leads to a devaluing of academic study or ecclesiastical status, and an emphasis on communitas suggests that they fit with the overall response to liminality which we have described.[24]

Stages of Development

Recognising that different countries will have developed at different paces we may say that the 'expressive revolution', as it has been termed, has passed through three phases. During the sixties it was largely the province of a counter-cultural elite and regarded by the masses at first with suspicion and even shock. During the seventies its ideals became much more generally acceptable and technological society even began to exploit it to its own ends, e.g., through the use of surrealist advertising. The other

---

24. On the charismatic movement see further, B. Martin *op. cit.*, 225f, W. Hollenweger, *The Pentecostals*, London, 1972, M. Poloma, *The Charismatic Movement*, Boston, 1982, M. Langley, 'Structure and Anti-Structure in the Churches: The Charismatic Movement' (unpublished paper), and B. Wilson, *Contemporary Transformations of Religion*, Oxford, 1976, 86f. Wilson says that just as credit cards have taken the waiting out of wanting so the charismatic movement has taken the waiting out of wanting on God.

feature of the seventies was that art, music and the theatre have a whole range of techniques and styles available to them all of which they used. There was no single expression, only a multiplicity of cries for experience. The sixties had opened Pandora's Box.

But by the eighties the limitations of the excessive concentration on experience began to be felt. Yankelovich argues that it could only flourish in a day of economic prosperity and the need to tighten the belt in recent years has called many to re-evaluate their expectations.[25] Bernice Martin argues that the quest for experience is not unlimited for a different reason. Before long the needs of instrumental society are bound to exercise a brake on the expressive revolution and order is reasserted.[26] There is good evidence of this in the political field in the UK and USA in terms of the election of Thatcher and Reagan to power, as well as in other fields such as art and education.

But there is a deeper reason for its limitation, too. The quest for narcissistic experience is full of deep ambiguity and disappointment. The ambiguity takes many forms but one principal manifestation of it lies in the fact that in spite of its search for communitas, it is a deeply selfish, alienating, anti-social, isolating and uprooting quest.[27] More important still is the fact that the quest for experience fails to satisfy. Mick Jagger of the Rolling Stones long ago sang 'I can't get no satisfaction'. And so it seems to be. Those who have indulged bear ample testimony to the spiritual desolation of so many of the quests for experience. Christopher Lasch documents, for example, the way in which so many biographies of the day declare that 'the

25. Yankelovich, *op. cit.*, pp. 206-215.
26. B. Martin, *op.cit.*, pp. 233-237.
27. See B. Martin, *op.cit.*, pp. 239, and P. Vitz, *op.cit.*, pp. 83. Yankelovich remains optimistic that it can lead to a new ethic of commitment but the evidence is to the contrary, *op. cit.*, pp. 244-264. Other commentators such as C. Lasch, *The Culture of Narcissism*, London, 1980, are deeply pessimistic.

voyage to the interior discloses nothing but a blank'.[28] The vacuum created is dangerous since men will be open to anything which promises to fill it.

It is sad to reflect that the optimism of this generation has led so quickly to disillusion. It reduces to the nursery rhyme:

> Old Mother Hubbard went to the cupboard
> To fetch her poor dog a bone,
> But when she got there the cupboard was bare
> And so her poor dog had none.

For all that, the experience of these last two and half decades is not to be dismissed. It has introduced inexorable, if somewhat modest, changes. Subjectivity, feeling, the quest for experience, anti-structure and communitas are here to stay and our theology must speak to them if it is to be relevant.

The Theological Implications

In conclusion, let us turn to some of the implications of our contemporary situation for the study of theology.

Firstly, we desperately need to consider the theology of experience. Our heritage from the Reformation onwards, through the Enlightenment and into the twentieth century has led us to emphasise the word, doctrine, right belief, and the cerebral aspects of the faith. Little attention has been paid to the theology of experience except by those such as Harvey Cox[29] or Morton Kelsey[30] who do not have an evangelical concern for Biblical truths. Indeed Kelsey shows how little attention is paid to the whole question of experience generally by theologians of whatever colour. It may be that our rejection of Schleiermacher and our fears about the woolliness of Otto have reinforced

28. Lasch, *op.cit.*, p. 21.
29. H. Cox, *The Seduction of the Spirit*, London, 1974.
30. M. Kelsey, *Encounter with God, a Theology of Christian Experience*, London, 1974.

our negative approach to the area. But these surely are precisely the reasons why an evangelical theology of experience ought to be constructed.

Perhaps James Dunn in *Jesus and the Spirit*[31] has made a start. There he considers not just the question of charismata in the early church but Jesus' experience of God in Sonship. Dunn points us in the right direction not only because he has put the topic on the agenda but because he does not limit his investigation to the 'peak experiences alone'. Our theology of experience ought not simply to concern itself with revelation, with the exceptional encounters of an Isaiah, with dramatic conversions and with baptism in the Spirit but also with the meaning of what it is to experience God daily.

Secondly, such an investigation must tackle a specific hermeneutical question – that of personality. It would be all too easy to read our contemporary understanding of personality as an individual subjective being back into the pages of Scripture. But if, as Malina has recently proposed,[32] the people of the first century knew nothing of such a personality but were instead dyadic personalities, that is those who perceived themselves in terms of what others perceived and fed back to them of information received outside themselves rather than from within then quick translations from the first to the twentieth century cannot be made.

Thirdly, attention must be given to what makes experience distinctively Christian. The quest for experience has broken down the boundaries between religious and secular experience so that many would describe rock or drugs or sex as a 'religious experience'. The boundaries have also been broken down between religions so that both the phenomenologists and the mass believe all religious experience to be the same whether it be Hindu or Christian

---

31. London, 1975.
32. B. Malina, *The New Testament World: Insights from Cultural Anthropology*, London, 1983, pp. 51-60.

charismatic. What distinguishes the Christian prophet or speaker in tongues from those who manifest similar phenomena but profess other faiths? Equally what do such experiences have in common with others?

Fourthly, we must engage in the obverse of that and have a contemporary theology of idolatry. The quest for experience, *per se*, may well be a cry for fulfillment in a world that has cut loose from its maker. But the cry often meets with a response which sets the plaintiff even further adrift. Today he so often does not even end up worshipping creation but worshipping himself. Narcissism must be the worst of all idolatries. The radical critique of idolatry must also take place within the church where the quest for experience may be a genuine hunger for God or may be just an expression of a wider bankrupt culture dressed up in Christian garb. Our critique therefore must take the form of Ephesians 4:17-24; where Paul not only exposes Gentile futility but tells the church that they must no longer live as the Gentiles do.

Fifthly, a further corollary is the need for a theology of order and structure. If it is true that 'in the course of history, an appeal to experience has often been made at times when men have felt oppressed by others and especially institutions' as Schillebeechz and Van Iersel[33] suggest, and the foregoing analysis would support, then no theology of experience is adequate unless it be in the context of a theology of order and structure. Deuteronomy 27:17 announces a curse on the man who moves his neighbour's boundary stone. But that is just what the quest for experience, manifest in the devotion to anti-structure, has done, not in literal terms but in moral, social and spiritual terms. Evangelicalism has tended to be a religion of the mind. The earlier decades of this century rightly saw it contending for the truth and therefore emphasising the reasonableness of its position, the veracity of Scripture, the reliability of the historical basis of the faith and the objectivity of faith as

33. *Concilium* 113, 1979, p. viii.

opposed to the subjectivity and unreliability of feelings. But the theatre of war has partially changed. Whilst those earlier battles cannot be forgotten and whilst the nature of cognition and truth remain paramount, new dimensions of warfare have entered which require us to consider a theology of experience. Elements from the tradition of pietism and the holiness movements need to be rediscovered. It is not an unbiblical concern. Our neglect of it is what is unbiblical. The Hebrews were a people who could *taste* and see that the Lord was good (Ps. 34:8). The church was composed of those who experienced the inbreaking of the kingdom of God with power and who not only passively witnessed but actively mediated the power of the Spirit (1 Cor. 4:20). And that is experience.

PROPHECY AND SPIRITUAL GIFTS THEN AND NOW[1]

MAX TURNER AND DAVID MACKINDER

In attempting to understand the nature and significance of 'spiritual gifts' one is forced to decide which end of the hermeneutical spectrum to start from. If one starts at the twentieth-century end, as some do, one inevitably runs the risk of reading first-century phenomena in the light of twentieth-century terms and categories – the vexed issue of the meaning of the phrase 'baptism in the Spirit' is a prime example. Alternatively one cannot attempt simply to bracket out twentieth-century concerns and categories by concentrating only on the first-century meaning and significance of the gifts. What I shall do in this essay is to focus primarily on *one* prototypical gift, the gift of prophecy. In order to understand this, and its related phenomena, we shall first examine the 'Spirit of prophecy' as articulated in Peter's sermon at Pentecost, then at the New Testament understanding of prophecy (concentrating mainly on Paul's understanding of it); after this I shall attempt to expound Paul's view about the significance of 'spiritual gifts' as given in 1 Corinthians 12-14. The second part of the essay will look at the points of correlation and difference between the New Testament understanding of 'spiritual gifts' and that found in today's Christian church.

---

1. This essay was originally written by M. M. B. Turner as a workshop paper for the 1984 conference of the Fellowship of European Evangelical Theologians and was subsequently published without revision in *Vox Evangelica* 15, 1985, pp. 7-64. It appears here in a greatly reduced and slightly revised form, though no changes have been made to its substance or conclusion: this abbreviation and revision was undertaken by D. Mackinder.

I. THE NEW TESTAMENT UNDERSTANDING OF SPIRITUAL GIFTS

1. Acts 2:16-39 and the 'Spirit of Prophecy'

The nature of the gift of the Spirit which Peter promises *to all* (Acts 2:38f.) on the day of Pentecost is significant. Contrary to Luke's view, this gift is often seen *either* as the beginning of the disciples' experience of the new age, the matrix of their Christian existence (so Dunn[2] and Bruner[3]), *or as* a *donum superadditum* of empowering (traditional Confirmationists and Pentecostalists). For Luke the disciples certainly recognized, enjoyed and preached the inbreaking kingdom of God within Jesus' ministry: forgiveness, table-fellowship with Jesus, and the renewing of their lives as they lived in discipleship to him[4] *were* their participation in the kingdom of God announced by Jesus. The passion and the ascension, however, posed a problem. Given their experience of God's rule in their discipleship to Jesus, and under the influence of the Spirit working through him, how would they continue to experience the powers of the new age when Jesus was removed into the heavenlies? John 14-16 provides the one answer: after the ascension the Spirit will be given to the disciples to act as their new Paraclete, and to bring them the presence of the Father and of the glorified Son (14:23).[5] Luke's

---

2. J. D. G. Dunn, *Baptism in the Holy Spirit*, London, 1970, *passim*, against which see M. M. B. Turner, *Luke and the Spirit: Studies in the Significance of Receiving the Spirit in Luke-Acts*, unpublished Ph.D., Cambridge, 1980, *passim* or, more briefly, Turner, 'Jesus and the Spirit in Lucan Perspective', *Tyn B* 32, 1981.
3. F. D. Bruner, *A Theology of the Holy Spirit*, London, 1970.
4. J. Jeremias, *New Testament Theology I*, London, 1971, *passim*; cf. Turner, *Luke and the Spirit*, chap. 3; 'Jesus and the Spirit', pp. 29-34.
5. As D. E. Holwerda, *The Holy Spirit and Eschatology in the Gospel of John*, Kampen, 1959; R. E. Brown, 'The Paraclete in the Fourth Gospel', NTS 13 (1966-7), pp. 113-32; see M. M. B.

answer, along very similar lines, lies in the gift of the Spirit at Pentecost *as the Spirit promised by Joel* (*cf.* Acts 2:17ff.).

Joel's promise is of the Spirit of prophecy, the organ of communication between God and a man enabling, *e.g.*, dreams, visions and words which are the basis of prophecy. In the OT it was a gift given to Moses, the seventy elders (Num. 11:16ff.), kings and prophets, to enable them to bring God's will and wisdom to the people. The eschatological hope of Jeremiah 31:34 was that one day *all* the Lord's people would know their God as directly. *It is this hope that Joel expresses in the form of a divine promise.* It was exactly *this* promise of the Spirit (*i.e.* as the Spirit of prophecy; the organ of communication between God and man) that was most widely expected in the Judaism of Jesus' day to be fulfilled at the eschaton. Any Jew listening to Peter's sermon would understand him to be promising just this – the only surprise being that *Jesus* was said to be at its *origin* (Acts 2:33). For Luke this solves the problem posed by the removal of Jesus in the ascension: for (by virtue of what is said in Acts 2:33) *Jesus can continue to exercise his lordship* in and through the disciples *through the Spirit of prophecy* acting as the organ of communication between the Father and Jesus in the heavenlies and the disciples on earth.[6]

Acts confirms this. Just as Joel's promised Spirit of prophecy was expected to bring God's revelation in *visions* and *dreams*, so in Acts we find the risen Lord giving such to the disciples; sometimes crucial theological visions (*cf.* Acts 10:10ff.); sometimes merely incidental personal direction (Acts 9:10ff.; 16:9ff.) or comfort (Acts 7:55f.; 18:9-10). Similarly, by the same gift, the risen Lord gives direction in *words* (without vision): *e.g.* 13:2; 10:19 *etc*. *Charismatic wisdom* and *discernment* are also given

---

Turner, 'The Significance of Receiving the Spirit in John's Gospel' *Vox Ev* 10, 1977, pp. 26-28.
6. Turner, *Luke and the Spirit*, chaps. 4, 5, for elucidation.

through the same Spirit of prophecy, as expected in Judaism (*cf.* the fulfilment of Lk. 21:15 in Acts 6:9-10, and *cf.* 5:3; 16:18 *etc.*). This last is closely associated with, and can result in, *power in preaching* – a major emphasis in Acts but *not* to be confused with the *essence* of the Pentecost gift. Power in preaching is merely one aspect of the activity of the Spirit as the christocentric Spirit of prophecy. Finally, of course, the Spirit *qua* Spirit of prophecy revealed himself in tongues – a form of inspired speech which Judaism would immediately recognize as belonging in the category of prophetism (*cf.* Acts 2:33 with its deterent in 2:4-6 and its explanation in 2:17-20).

Clearly, *after* the ascension, this gift promised by Peter is a *sine qua non* of Christian existence: the means of on-going knowledge of the Lord. Any man experiencing the phenomena noted above owes them to the Spirit experienced as what Luke means by Joel's promised Spirit of prophecy. *Equally clearly*, however, the character of the gift Luke envisages virtually guarantees that he expected visions, dreams, prophecy *etc.* to be *continuing* phenomena. Not a few exegetes have dismissed such gifts as merely the dispensable *signs* of the presence of the Spirit. But this is a misunderstanding: according to what Peter says such gifts *correspond to the essential character* of the Spirit as the Spirit of prophecy: they are instances of the Spirit acting as the organ of communication of God's revelation to a man, enabling him to receive Jesus' word and direction.

Having sketched Luke's understanding of the meaning of the gift of the Spirit of prophecy, let us turn now to the New Testament understanding of the phenomenon of prophecy itself.

2. The New Testament Understanding of Prophecy

(a) Paul's understanding of prophecy
Prophecy in the New Testament church has been the subject of many works, the most significant of which are those

by E. Fascher,[7] É. Cothonet,[8] T. M. Crone,[9] G. Dautzenberg,[10] V. Müller,[11] J. Panagopoulos, [12] E. E. Ellis,[13] D. Hill,[14] W. Grudem,[15] and D. E. Aune,[16] whose work surpasses anything so-far written on the subject. With the works of Grudem and Aune we arrive at some precision on the question of what 'prophecy' meant in the New Testament, and generally in its environment. Essentially 'prophecy' fell within the sphere of what the ancients called 'natural divination' (as opposed to 'technical divination'):[17] it 'is a specific form of divination that consists of intelligible verbal messages believed to originate with God and communicated through inspired human intermediaries'.[18] Similarly, Grudem can insist that the essence of prophecy, for Paul, is to be inferred from 1 Corinthians 14:29f, where Paul states: 'Two or three prophets should speak and the others should weigh care-

7. E. Fascher, *Prophetes*: *Eine sprach – und religionsgeschichtliche Untersuchung*, Geissen, 1927.
8. É. Cothonet, 'Prophétisme dans le nouveau Testament', *DBSupp* 8, pp. 1222-1337.
9. T. M. Crone, *Early Christian Prophecy: A Study of its Origin and Function*, Baltimore, 1973.
10. G. Dautzenberg, *Urchristliche Prophetie*, Stuttgart, 1975.
11. U. Müller, *Prophetie und Predigt im Neuen Testament*, Gütersloh, 1975, for a critique of whose method see J. Panagopoulos (ed.), *Prophetic Vocation in the New Testament and Today*, Leiden, 1977, pp. 3-5.
12. Panagopoulos, *ibid.*
13. E. E. Ellis, *Prophecy and Hermeneutic*, Tübingen, 1978.
14. D. Hill, *New Testament Prophecy*, London, 1979.
15. W. Grudem, *The Gift of Prophecy in 1 Corinthians*, Washington, 1982.
16. D. E. Aune, *Prophecy in Early Christianity and the Ancient Mediterranean World*, Grand Rapids, 1983.
17. Aune, *ibid.* p. 339, *cf.* p. 23f., p. 35ff.
18. *Ibid.* p. 339 Aune is aware of the qualifications that need to be made with respect to Delphic prophecy (where Pythia may utter *un*intelligible prophecy *interpreted* by the *prophetes*) and to Qumran writings (where the Teacher of Righteousness regards himself as an eschatological prophet but does not prophesy as such) see chap. 2 and p. 132ff., and p. 241ff. respectively.

fully what is said. And if a revelation comes to someone who is sitting down, the first should stop. For you can all prophesy in turn so that everyone may be instructed and encouraged.' Grudem elucidates this (at length) to mean that for Paul prophecy is the reception and *subsequent* communication of spontaneous divinely given *apokalypsis*.[19] A question remains as to whether Paul uses the designation 'prophet' of anyone who *once* 'prophesies', or restricts it in some way. Grudem may be right to argue that Paul can use the term *both* ways (*cf.* 1 Cor. 14:32), but usually restricted it in a manner that involved both subjective factors (*cf.* 1 Cor. 14:37: 'If anyone considers himself to be a prophet ... ') and *informal* recognition by the church.[20]

(b) The Understanding of Prophecy in Luke-Acts
What Luke has to say is roughly in accord with this. In Luke 22:64, Jesus, blindfolded, is mocked: 'Prophesy! Who hit you?' The assumption, in accord with the above, is that God could reveal the identity of the assailant, and Jesus declare it (*cf.* Lk. 7:39): this process would be 'prophecy'. A similar picture emerges in Acts 2:17f. quoting Joel. Israel's sons and daughters will prophesy (17b and 18b) because God will reveal things to them in dreams and visions – the assumption (in accord with most Old Testament and much intertestamental literature) is that prophecy is the declaring of a revelatory experience. In Acts 19:6 Luke describes an illapse of the Spirit on twelve 'disciples' at Ephesus with the words 'they began to speak in tongues and prophesy'. Here 'prophesy' probably does *not* have the sense 'to report a revelation (word, vision or dream) received', but 'to speak while under the external influence of the Spirit'. The precedents for that type of 'prophecy' are to be found in I Samuel 19:20-24; 10:5-13; Numbers 11:24-30 *etc.* What is not clear is whether the

19. Grudem, *Gift*, pp. 115-143, especially p. 139ff.
20. Grudem, *Gift*, chap. 4 especially p. 23.

kai is epexegetic (thereby identifying the speaking in tongues as 'prophecy' – which would certainly be consistent with general Greek usage) or conjoining. But either way we have a different sense from that which Paul uses in the situation confronting him at Corinth.

(c) The New Testament Concepts of Prophecy: Further Consideration

If the essence of prophecy in Paul and Luke-Acts is, as we have noted, the declaration of a revelation imparted by a spiritual agent (God, or Jesus, in Spirit in the case of true prophets/prophecies),[21] what can we discern about the nature of New Testament prophecy beyond what we have said above? Six major points require elucidation:

The psychology of prophecy.[22] The sharp antithesis drawn between Greco-Roman 'ecstatic' prophecy on the one hand, and Jewish and Christian 'controlled' prophecy on the other, seems to rest on a caricature of the former.[23] Nevertheless, Grudem and Aune are probably right to insist that we do not encounter ecstatic[24] prophecy in the New Testament (not even behind 1 Cor. 12:3),[25] but what Aune describes as 'controlled' prophetic 'trance' (using and developing the anthropological typology of E. Bourguinon

21. Not by 'angels' as Ellis supposes; see Grudem, *Gift*, pp. 120-22.
22. See Grudem, *Gift*, chap. 2 onwards.
23. *Contra*, especially Bacht, see Aune, *Prophecy* 230 and *passim* for arguments.
24. 'Ecstasy is much too vague a term to employ unless it be abundantly qualified to make clear that there are too many degrees of it, ranging from mild dissociation to extreme uncontrollable rapture', C. G. Williams, 'Glossolalia as a Religious Phenomenon: "Tongues" at Corinth and Pentecost', *Religion* 5, 1975, 21; see further his *Tongues of the Spirit: A Study of Pentecostal Glossolalia and Related Phenomena*, Cardiff, 1981, chap. 1.
25. Grudem, *Gift*, pp.150-77, especially pp. 155-72; K. Hemphill, *The Pauline Concept of Charisma* (unpublished Ph.D., Cambridge 1976) pp. 69-72.

and the sociological analysis of I. M. Lewis.)[26] On the one hand the revelation that comes to the prophet is distinct and compelling, such that the prophet may (wrongly in Paul's opinion) feel he could not resist the Spirit (1 Cor. 14:32) or (rightly in Paul's view) that he must be given almost immediate hearing if the revelation comes to him during worship (1 Cor. 14:30). On the other hand he is sufficiently aware of his surroundings to be able to bring his speech to a close when another signals he has received an immediate revelation (1 Cor. 14:30). The strength and sharpness of the revelation probably varied widely. At one extreme we have the powerful visionary experiences of Paul, *e.g.* in 2 Corinthians 12[27] (though not all led to prophecy), or John in the Apocalypse (note John characterizes his work as *prophecy*: Rev. 1:3; 22:18ff.): at the other extreme *apokalyptein* can be used even of the firm conviction gradually etched on the mind (*e.g.* Phil. 3:15). The verb is neutral with respect to the strength and clarity of the revelation.[28]

The content of prophetic speech. This seems to have been wideranging; from specific directions to churches concerning personnel (Acts 13:2f.), the solution of disputes (Acts 15:28,32), specific guidance and assurance given to missionaries (*e.g.* Acts 16:6ff.), and warning of famine (Acts 11:28), to prediction of Paul's personal fate (Acts 20:23; 21:11). It should be noted that each of these instances involves the necessity of God's revealing particularistic knowledge — not merely general principles that could be deduced, for example, by illuminated reading of the Torah, or from the gospel tradition, or from apostolic *didache*. The prophetic analysis of the seven churches in Revelation 1-3 points in the same direction. Paul, too, assumes that the

26. Aune, *Prophecy*, pp. 19-21
27. *Cf.* A. T. Lincoln, '"Paul the Visionary": The Setting and Significance of the Rapture to Paradise in 2 Corinthians XII, 1-10' *NTS* 25, 1979, pp. 204ff.
28. Grudem, *Gift*, pp. 134-6.

same particularistic knowledge will be imparted when he says the outsider will be convicted, for God (through Corinthian prophesying) will reveal the secrets of his heart (1 Cor. 14:23). What is envisaged here is the laying bare of personal information which the outsider is convinced only God could have revealed (as in Jn. 4:16ff.).[29] But it is unlikely that Paul would have placed prophecy in such a privileged position (prophets second to apostles; prophecy the highest gift to which the Corinthians could aspire: 1 Cor. 12:28f.; 14:1 *etc.*) unless prophetic *apokalypsis* went further than this, and involved the impartation of doctrinal 'mysteries' (*cf.* 1 Cor. 13:2).[30] Aune uses five criteria to identify prophetic oracles in the New Testament (all or most to be satisfied before a passage is recognized as 'prophecy').[31] Prophecy may be suspected if a saying or speech is (1) attributed to a supernatural being; (2) consists of prediction or involves special knowledge; (3) introduced or concluded by formula(e) which in other contexts are marks of prophetic diction; (4) prefixed by a statement of the inspiration of the speaker; (5) does not sit easily in the literary context. Using these criteria Aune discovers some fifty-nine prophecies embedded in the New Testament (*e.g.* 2 Cor. 12:9; 1 Cor. 15:51f.; Rom. 11:25f.; Thess. 4:15f.; Gal. 5:21; 1 Thess. 3:4; 4:2-6; 2 Thess. 3:6, 10, 12 from among the Paulines).[32] The types of oracle include *oracles of assurance* (Acts 18:9; 23:11; 27: 23-24; 2 Cor. 12:9); *prescriptive oracles* (Gal. 5:21; Acts 13:2; 21:4; Thess. 3:6 *etc.*); *announcements of salvation* (Rev. 14:13; 19:9 *etc.*); *announcements of judgements* (Acts 13:9-11; 1 Cor. 14:37f.; Gal. 1:8-9); *legitimation oracles*(*e.g.* 1 Cor. 12:3 – and including *self-commendation oracles* (Rev. 1:8, 17)) and *eschatological theophany oracles* (Rom. 11:25f.; 1 Cor. 15:51f.; 1 Thess. 4:16f., *etc.*).

29. See E. Best, 'Prophets and Preachers', *SJT* 12, 1959, p. 146ff.
30. Dautzenberg, *Urchristliche*, chap. 4.
31. Aune, *Prophecy*, p. 247f, p. 317f.
32. *Ibid.*, chap. 10.

Clearly the last of these – and for that matter the previous three types – are heavily doctrinal in nature.[33]

It should be obvious by now that the form and content of early Christian prophecy was exceedingly varied and parallels can be found to some forms in non-prophetic speech. This observation prompts Aune to his conclusion: 'the distinctive feature of prophetic speech was not so much its *content* or *form*, but its [direct] *supernatural origin*'.[34]

The purpose(s) of prophecy. On this it is commonplace to begin with Paul's statement in 1 Corinthians 14:3 (*cf.* 31) that prophecy is for the edification, exhortation and consolation of the congregation. Two points must be remembered however. First, Paul does not offer this proposition as a sufficient condition of the predicate *propheteia*. It is not: forms of speech other than prophecy serve the same purpose, such as homily, exposition and teaching. These alternatives may be highly charismatic too; but that does not make them prophecy.[35] Second, Paul's statement in 14:3 need not even be a *necessary* condition of *propheteuein* – he may merely have thought it would usually characterize congregational prophecy. Certainly 1 Corinthians 14:3 should not be used to marginalize prophecy given to individuals *outside* the framework of the assembly of the congregation (as e.g. Agabus to Paul in Acts 21:11).[36] More precisely, the function of prophecy can to some extent be read off the forms of prophetic speech identified: oracles of assurance, salvation, judgement, legitimation, prescription and eschatological theophany *etc*. These activities of God in the congregation serve as a sign (*cf.* 1 Cor. 14:22) to his people: a sign of blessing indicating that he is with them; that he knows them intimately; that he knows what dangers beset them;

---

33. *Ibid.*, chaps. 10, 12.
34. *Ibid.*, p. 338.
35. See especially Grudem, *Gift*, pp. 181-5.
36. Aune, *Prophecy*, p. 195ff., p. 211ff.

that he has them in his hand, leads them and instructs them. It is a sign that is transparent, too, to the unbeliever (vv. 24f.).

Does prophecy denote charismatic exegesis, preaching or teaching? It need not be doubted that prophecies had didactic and prescriptive elements (see above),[37] nor that those who rose to be recognised as 'prophets' in the early church were able to preach and to teach. But it is quite another matter to assert that inspired preaching, exegesis or teachings are actually (wholly or in part) what the New Testament *means* by prophecy. Warnings against such misunderstandings, which are especially prevalent in Reformed circles, have been given by (*inter multos alios*) Best[38] and Grudem.[39] But the positive case has recently been reasserted by Cothonet,[40] Hill[41] and Ellis.[42] Antecedently the latter position looks unlikely. After all, prophecy in the Greco-Roman world was *oracular* speech or writing.[43] And in Judaism the belief was widespread that *prophecy* had ceased; *now* there were *sages* and *scribes*.[44] Where such statements are made, the point is precisely that God no longer speaks *directly, but by scripture* interpreted and expounded. Where such statements are denied, and the continuation of prophecy maintained, it is invariably as *oracular* speech; the declaration of knowledge imparted directly to the speaker from a supernatural source.[45] As Christians spoke of *two* charismata – teaching *and* prophecy (*cf.* 1 Cor. 12:28 *etc.*) – it is antecedently

37. However, see Grudem, *Gift*, p. 185ff, on *manthano* in 1 Cor. 14:32.
38. Best, 'Prophets' *passim*.
39. Grudem, *Gift*, p. 139ff.
40. Panagopoulos, *Prophetic Vocation*, p. 77ff.
41. *Ibid.*, p. 108ff. (with modifications and reservations).
42. Ellis, *Prophecy and Hermeneutic* pt. 2.
43. Aune, *Prophecy*, chap. 2.
44. Grudem,*Gift* 21ff. and Aune, *Prophecy*, chap. 5 for full treatment and literature.
45. Aune, *ibid.*, p. 141ff., p. 144ff.

probable that the old and widespread distinction holds. Charismatic *teaching* includes exposition that relates scripture and tradition to the immediate needs of a congregation, while prophecy primarily denotes the declaration by a man of material revealed to him *directly* by the supernatural source rather than mediated through consideration of scripture.[46]

Those who argue for the equation of prophecy with preaching usually argue from the paraenetic function of Old Testament prophecy to the conclusion that New Testament paraenetic is therefore prophecy; but paraenetic is not a distinctive feature of Old Testament prophecy as such, rather it is common to a variety of genres. The more subtle case, made by Ellis, that the New Testament evinces occasions where midrashic exegesis is accompanied by the formula 'says the Lord' and that the latter is a claim to prophetic knowledge by the exegete (*e.g.* Rom. 12:19's use of Dt. 32:35) has been severely criticized by Aune.[47] Aune counters (1) that the same phenomena in *Barnabas* are explained by the writer not as *prophecy* but as *teaching*; (2) that the *legei kyrios* formula is not a claim to inspired speech (and anyway never evinced in prophetic speech) but simply identifies God as the speaker of the Old Testament passage under consideration and (3) that there is no material (historical) connection between such 'implicit midrash' and early Christian prophecy as such; *no evidence connects charismatic exegesis with prophets*, while such teaching would naturally be expected of 'teachers'. The burden of proof seems to rest with those who wish to claim that charismatic and expository preaching were aspects of prophecy rather than teaching.

Were all regarded as able to prophesy? We can be certain that in Paul's view not all were prophets: the form of the question in 1 Corinthians 12:29 ensures that. But it

---
46. *Ibid.*, pp. 339-46.
47. *Ibid.*, pp. 343-5

has usually been argued that Paul, and others in the New Testament, reserved the honoured title 'prophet' for the recognized *specialist* in prophecy, while allowing that all at Corinth might prophesy one-by-one (1 Cor. 14:31).[48] To this is usually added the further argument that, in Luke, the gift of the Spirit described and promised in Acts 2 is Joel's promise of the Spirit of prophecy. *Ergo*, it is all too often concluded, each Christian is a prophet, or, at least, can prophesy. I agree with the stated premise (and elsewhere have defended the position at length);[49] but the conclusion is most unsure. The Spirit of prophecy as understood by Judaism was the organ of revelation and communication between God and a man. So the Spirit of prophecy (failing some alternative agency) was a necessary condition of prophesying – but in Luke's view (again following, but also developing Jewish understanding) the Spirit of prophecy might indeed give gifts such as dreams, visions, words of guidance *etc.* (which are the basis of prophecy), but also gave other *related* charismata such as tongues, charismatic wisdom, power in evangelizing and pastoral preaching *etc.*[50] Now Luke almost certainly regarded this diversity of gifts as coming under the general title 'prophetism' (prophecy and *related* phenomena), but it is a moot point whether he would have called all these gifts *prophecy as such*; certainly there is no evidence that he does. One cannot show that by the term prophecy he means anything other than oracular speech (controlled or ecstatic – possibly including tongues *cf.* Acts 19:6); and it would be very difficult indeed to show that Luke believed

48. See Turner, *Luke and the Spirit*, p. 131f. for literature.
49. Turner, *Ibid.*, chaps. 4, 5; 'Spirit Endowment in Luke-Acts: Some Linguistic Considerations' *Vox Ev.* 12, 1981, pp. 55-60. For a survey of scholars' views on what receiving the Spirit means in Luke-Acts see Turner, 'The Significance of Receiving the Spirit in Luke-Acts: A survey of Modern Scholarship', *Trin J* 2, 1981, pp. 131-58.
50. Turner, *Luke and the Spirit*, pp. 134-46; 'Jesus and the Spirit' pp. 38-40.

all Christians prophesied in the narrow sense. At most we can say that, as the Spirit at Pentecost is the Spirit of prophecy, Luke may have expected that many, or even the majority of Christians, would be able to prophesy. We may now return to the Pauline evidence. Aune has pointed out that 'all may prophesy one-by-one' could simply denote the prophets. In which case there is no suggestion that prophecy is universal. However, it is probably better, with Grudem, to take a middle position. Prophets are the tested specialists; all may *seek* prophecy (1 Cor. 14:1,5,39), for none are excluded *a priori*, but God will not in fact distribute any one gift to all (1 Cor. 12:14-30).[51]

The authority and limitations of New Testament prophecy. The canonical prophets are represented as having spoken in the name of the Lord as his messengers; their words were neither more nor less than what God had commanded them to utter. A man might test the prophet, but he could not tamper with the oracle once he decided the prophet was authentic. To disobey such a prophet was to disobey God. Correspondingly, should the prophet be shown to have erred in any respect in his prophecy the sanction was death. The seriousness of disobedience or of prophesying falsely underscored that the oracles of the prophets were the very words of God, holy and authoritative. Such is the picture fleshed out by several scholars, and at its most nuanced in Grudem. In the New Testament, as Grudem, following writers such as Guy and Friedrich, sees it, the mantle of prophecy with authority of actual words transfers to the apostles,[52] and the more widespread phenomenon of New Testament prophecy carries only the authority of general content: it is parallel to the revelatory phenomena in early Judaism with its con-

---

51. Grudem, *Gift*, pp. 235ff.
52. *Ibid.*, chap. 1 especially pp. 43-45; similarly Hill, *NT Prophecy*, *e.g.* p. 116.

sciousness of the withdrawal of true prophecy – a weaker sort of prophecy with a lesser authority.[53] The evidence on which this sort of construct is based is (1) many aspects of Paul's apostolic self-consciousness closely parallel that of Old Testament prophets.[54] (2) Paul relativizes the authority of Corinthian prophets and subordinates them to his(1 Cor. 14:37f.), (3) John – an apostle – claims divine authority of actual words for the Apocalypse (Rev. 22:18f). (4) Paul knows that prophecy is sometimes so unprepossessing that prophecy as a whole is in danger of being despised (1 Thess. 5:19f.). (5) Both at Thessalonika and at Corinth he demands that prophecy be *evaluated*[55] – not that it just be accepted totally as true prophecy or rejected totally as false prophecy (as in the Old Testament, according to Grudem). The presupposition is that any one New Testament prophetic oracle is expected to be mixed in quality, and the wheat must be separated from the chaff. The prophet may genuinely have received something from God (albeit often indistinctly), but the 'vision' is partial, limited in perspective, and prone to wrong interpretation by the prophet even as he declares it (1 Cor. 13:12).

This presentation of Grudem's case is vastly oversimplified, but we suspect that Grudem, too, has occasionally himself over-schematized the evidence. The sharp distinction between apostolic and merely prophetic prophecy seems to be overdrawn. Undoubtedly the apostles were recognized (at least in some circles) to be commissioned with the Lord's authority – but *were* they regarded as

---

53. Grudem, *Gift*, p. 21ff., pp. 54-73.
54. See especially J. M. Myers and E. D. Freed, 'Is Paul also among the Prophets?' *Int*.20, 1966, pp. 40-53, but see also the criticism by Aune, *Prophecy, p.* 206ff., p. 275ff: Dautzenberg, *Urchristliche*, p. 126-48.
55. For this sense of *diakrino* (*contra* Dautzenberg) see Grudem, *Gift*, pp. 263-88.

PROPHECY AND SPIRITUAL GIFTS

Yahweh's prophetic messengers giving his *actual words*?[56] I see no evidence to suggest such outside the Apocalypse and even *there* the claim to authority is made in the name of *prophecy* not of apostolicity.[57] All that Paul says is consistent with his believing he has rather full 'authority of general content' (*i.e.* it has a true propositional structure), but nowhere does he suggest that he is claiming 'divine authority of actual words'. This is where Grudem's distinction breaks down (and he is not unaware of the problems): semantically it is not the surface structure of the wording, but the semantic structure of the propositions of communication that is primarily significant. And this suggests what seems reasonable on other grounds too, namely, that there was no *sharp* distinction between apostolic prophecy and prophets' prophesyings – rather, a spectrum of authority of charisma extending from apostolic speech and prophecy (backed by apostolic commission) at one extreme, to vague and barely profitable attempts at oracular speech such as brought 'prophecy' as a whole into question at Thessalonika (1 Thess. 5:19f.) at the other. A prophet's speech might fall anywhere on the spectrum, so

---

56. Paul's authority, as Dunn rightly observes, *Jesus and the Spirit,* p. 47, was primarily the authority of the gospel itself as it was revealed to Paul in the Damascus Road christophany; *cf.*, J. C. Beker, *Paul the Apostle,* Edinburgh, 1980, S. Kim, *The Origin of Paul's Gospel* Tübingen, 1981. Paul's references to 'my gospel' certainly do not seem to me to necessitate a belief that Paul claimed divine authority of actual words (*contra* Grudem). It is the general structure of his gospel that he hereby denotes.
57. See the critique of Aune, *Prophecy,* 206-8.

the task of evaluation fell on the congregation.[58] The New Testament surely was not claiming that the Old Testament Spirit of prophecy had now returned, but merely to the apostles – thus dividing all other persons or charismata off and levelling them down with the sort of phenomena professed by early Judaism in its consciousness that the Spirit had been withdrawn (Acts 2:17-38). Paul does not say that all New Testament prophets see through a glass darkly while apostles see clearly; the apostles' prophecy, too, is *ek merous* and *en ainigmati* (1 Cor. 13:12).[59]

Let us now turn to an examination of Paul's argument about the value and status of spiritual gifts in the Corinthian church, as detailed in 1 Corinthians 12-14.

3. Paul's Teaching on Spiritual Gifts in 1 Corinthians 12-14[60]

In 1 Corinthians 12:1-7 Paul lists six characteristics that spiritual gifts have in common: (1) they are *energemata* ('workings') of God (v. 6) (2) they are *diakoniai* ('acts of service') related to the Lord (as agent? as beneficiary?) (v. 5) (3) they are *phaneroseis* ('manifestations') of the Spirit

---

58. On the importance of congregational discernment for Paul, see especially J. D. G. Dunn, 'Discernment of Spirits - A Neglected Gift' in W. Harrington (ed) *Witness to the Spirit*, Dublin, 1979, pp. 79-96 and more fully 'The Responsible Congregation (1 Cor. 14: 26-40)' in L. de Lorenzi (ed) *Charisma und Agape* (1 Ko 10-14), Rome, 1983, pp. 201-36; *cf.* J. Martucci, '*Diakrisis pneumaton* (1 Co 12, 10)' *Eg Th* 9, 1978, pp.465-71 and J. Gnilka, 'La Relation entre la Responsibilité Communautaire et l'Autorité Ministérielle d'apres le NT, en Tenant Compte Spécialement du "Corpus Paulinum"' in L. de Lorenzi, *Paul de Tarse: Apôtre du Notre Temps*, Rome, 1979, pp. 455-70.
59. As Grudem himself notes, *Gift*, p. 53f., p. 49, n. 100.
60. For an outline of the problems relating to these chapters see the introductory essay by Dupont, 'Dimensions du problème des charismes dans 1 Co. 12-14' and all the essays in De Lorenzi, *Charisma und Agape*.

(v. 7) and so (4) *pneumatika* (1, probably, *cf.* 14:1); (5) for the common good: *i.e.* of the church (v. 7) and, finally (6) they are *charismata* given *by* the Spirit (vv. 4, 8),[61] In 12:1-3 he broadens what was probably a narrow Christian view of who were *pneumatikos* – pointing out that all who affirm 'Jesus is Lord' do so by the Spirit,[62] and so, in a sense, are spiritual. He then interprets the Corinthian *pneumatikos* terminology in the light of a theme already given importance earlier in the epistle, that of *grace* (*charis*: 1:4-7; 3:10). Accordingly, '*pneumatika*' is replaced by '*charismata*' (v. 4 – until he can safely switch back at 14:1), and manifestations of the Spirit are thus presented to the Corinthians as concrete results and activities of God's universally bestowed *charis*. As such they are not the objects of prideful boasting.

Paul's list of gifts in 12:8-10 is not a neutral one but reflects (1) the interest of the Corinthians in the spectacular and (2) his preparation for his specific pastoral advice on the manner and practice of gifts in 1 Corinthians 13-14; issues which have been raised by the Corinthian letter to him.

After briefly characterizing the gifts of the Spirit in verses 4-7, and listing them in verses 8-10, Paul maintains that the Spirit distributes the gifts to each as he wills. The *hekasto*(i) of verses 7, 11 are still ambiguous: does the Spirit distribute to each who will receive *charisma*, or is Paul saying that each Christian receives some gift? So far the Corinthians could read the letter on the assumption that *charismata/pneumatika* denote only the sort of gifts listed in verses 8-10, and that Paul is only talking about the Spirit's work among an inner circle of *pneumatikoi*.[63] But that he is not becomes clear in 12:12-

---

61. Dunn, *Jesus and the Spirit*, p. 37 and p. 38.
62. See Grudem, *Gift* p. 156-73 especially p. 170ff; Hemphill, *Pauline Concept of Charisma*, p. 68ff.
63. For the view that Paul does *not* believe all have gifts see the list of writers in U. Brockhaus, *Charisma und Amt*, Wuppertal, 1975, p. 204, n. 3.

31. He starts with the insistence that the Spirit has made *all* members one body and that all are made to drink (or be watered by) the same Spirit. The body imagery not only allows him to insist on the need for diversity making up the one unity, but permits him also to raise the possibility that the parts of the body that seem weaker, less honourable, or less presentable, may prove indispensable and more honoured (vv. 22-24), God giving greater honour to the 'inferior' part. Paul is preparing to say that some divine workings which the Corinthians have played down are in fact of greater significance than the list of highly prized items in verses 8-10.

The trap is now sprung in verses 28-31. In verse 18 Paul had spoken of God setting the members in the body, and earlier still he had spoken of *all* being gifted – but the precise range of 'members', or 'gifts', was unclear. Now in verses 28-31 it is spelt out. God has set in the church (v. 28 *cf.* v. 18) *first* apostles, *then* prophets, *then* teachers *etc.* – a listing which immediately gives priority to leadership which some of the Corinthians were wont to downplay (*cf.* 1 Cor. 1-4; 16:15-16). Paul is pointing out that these functions, too, are grounded in *charismata* (v. 31). The abilities enabling teachers *etc.* to function are no less 'spiritual' than those vaunted by the self-styled *pneumatikoi*. Under the same rubric comes 'helps' (*antilempseis*) and 'administrations' (*kybernesis*), which the Corinthian enthusiasts probably did not reckon among 'God's workings' at all; these may well have been what Paul had in mind when he introduced the 'unseemly' and the 'weak' members earlier. These, too, God 'set' in the church, and by the *charis* they received, their functions, as well, are to be characterized as the outworking of *charisma*. So Paul broadens out the notion of the locus of the Spirit's work, and can finish 'seek the greater *charismata*' – presumably excluding that which enables apostleship, ranked first, but certainly *not* excluding that which gave access to the second in rank, the *propheteia* encouraged in chapter 14, and which constitutes one *prophetes* (v. 28).

Chapter 13 does not attempt to marginalize the issue of gifts, but to state the manner in which the genuine *pneumatikos* exercises the gifts [64] – in love, for the upbuilding of the church (and it is precisely the *charismata* that build up most which constitute the greater gifts to be sought)[65] – and this is spelt out in practical terms in chapter 14.[66]

Though initially suggesting a narrow range of denotata for the term charismata – namely the dramatic demonstrations of the Spirit – by the end of the discourse Paul has demanded a totally different perspective; one that recognizes even the allegedly 'mundane' services performed in the body of Christ as God's work, as *charismata*, and manifestations of the Spirit.[67] It is not (as Dunn would have it) that Paul is saying *striking* acts of administration or 'help' are *charismata, because* they demonstrate the Spirit's work; but rather that even ordinary 'weak' services that are 'not honoured' are perceived by the spiritual man as God's work; as *charis* individuated as *charisma*.

(a) Charismata in Paul
Do the words *pneumatika* and *charismata* function as semi-technical terms for what Pentecostalism and the Charismatic movement[68] has called 'supernatural spiritual

64. Hemphill, *Pauline Concept of Charisma* 100; S. Lyonnet 'Agapè et Charismes selon 1 Co 12, 31' De Lorenzi, *Paul de Tarse*, pp. 509-27.
65. Hemphill, *ibid.*, pp. 97-122.
66. For the argument of chap. 14 see L. Hartman, '1 Co. 14, 1-25; Argument and Some Problems' in De Lorenzi, *Charisma und Agape*, pp. 149-69.
67. Hemphill, *Pauline Concept of Charisma,* pp. 82-92; *cf.* Brockhaus, *Charisma und Amt*, p.204, 'Die Korinther engten den Kreis der Pneumatiker ein; Paulus weitet ihn aus.'
68. For attitudes in this sector see, for example, Bruner, *A Theology of the Holy Spirit,* chap. 4; W.J. Hollenweger, *The Pentecostals,* London, 1972, chap. 25; M. Poloma, *The Charismatic Movement,* Boston, 1982, Pt. 2 especially chaps. 4, 5; J. I.

gifts'? The attempt to make the word semi-technical could only succeed if a fairly strict stereotype could be offered. Grau and Dunn have tried to give this by defining *charisma* strictly in terms of *energema* (1 Cor. 12:6) or *praxis* (Rom. 12:4).[69] For Dunn this means that in Paul *charismata* are 'concrete actions, actual events, not . . . latent possibilities and hidden talents'.[70] Consequently, only particular occasions of teaching, leadership, pastoralia *etc.*, or specific *events* of prophecy, tongues *etc.*, can be *charismata*. If we restrict our analysis to 1 Corinthians 12:8-10, Dunn's gloss on Paul may seem appropriate. But to force it on his broader list of charismata in 1 Corinthians 12:28f., and Romans 12:6ff., so that only what we might in twentieth-century terms designate as 'strongly charismatic' *acts* (of leadership, administration, help *etc.*) are accounted *charismata*, seems totally unjustified. Hemphill rightly criticizes Dunn's formulations of the antithesis as between either activities of the Spirit in the moment or latent possibilities and hidden talents. There is room for middle ground – especially concerning activities which demand a wide range of competence such as leadership or pastoralia. Could not Paul speak of an ability possessed, which was recognized and dedicated to God, and used for the upbuilding of the church (even recognized ultimately as being the work of a God who fashions man from the womb) as *charisma* (*cf.* 1 Cor. 7:7!)? As Hemphill points out, if Paul thought of *charismata* merely as momentary activities of the Spirit he could effectively have quenched all Corinthian boasting by saying no-one *possesses* any gifts. But in fact

---

Packer, *Keep in Step with the Spirit*, Leicester, 1984, chap.5. Unfortunately A. Mather's *Theology of the Charismatic Movement in Britain from 1964 to the Present Day* (unpublished Ph.D., University College of North Wales, 1982) came to my attention too late to be used, but see her article 'Talking Points: The Charismatic Movement' *Themelios* 9, 1984, pp.17-21.

69. *Contra* F. Grau, *Der neutestamentliche Begriff* (unpublished Ph.D., Tübingen, 1946), see Hemphill, *Ibid.*, p. 187, n. 77.
70. Dunn, *Jesus and the Spirit*, p. 209.

PROPHECY AND SPIRITUAL GIFTS

he speaks freely of people 'having' gifts, and gives practical instructions for utilizing the gift one 'has' (ch. 14) – indeed *charismata* can only threaten the community at all if they are 'possessed in stewardship' (*cf.* 1 Pet. 4:10) and hence subject to immature *misuse* by the one who 'has' the gift.[71] We conclude that 'charisma' has a much broader *sense* than the narrowly restricted one Dunn and Grau attempt to force on it, and we doubt whether the designation 'semi-technical' can be justified.

Charisma also has a correspondingly wider denotation than is often assumed. While Paul enumerates *nine* gifts in 1 Corinthians 12:8-10, he widens the class considerably in 1 Corinthians 12:28ff.; Romans 12:6-8 and Ephesians 4:11f. The lists are clearly *ah hoc* and incomplete and they suggest that for Paul virtually anything that can be viewed as God's enabling of a man for the upbuilding of the church could and would be designated a *charisma*, if Paul's purpose was to underline its nature as *given* by God.

(b) One 'Gift' Per Christian?

One might think that in 1 Corinthians 12:7-11 Paul is saying each member of the body receives just one type of spiritual gift. But such a view would misunderstand Paul. Certainly the church is to be characterized by a variety of gifts, and these will be distributed in such a way that individual members of Christ are dependent on each other – but this must not be made to suggest either that each is a specialist with just one operation of the Spirit, or, worse, that the Spirit's distribution of gifts involves a different allocation of types of *charismata* each time the assembly meets. The broad sense Paul attributes to '*charismata*' allows him to use it at different levels. He actually speaks of individual instances of healings in the plural as *charismata iamaton* (1 Cor. 12:9), but he might *equally* have said *allo(i) charisma iamaton*, using the singular, and thereby summing up all the specific instances generally as God's

---

71. Hemphill, *Pauline Concept of Charisma*, p. 78, n. 92.

gracious enabling. Similarly he could have spoken of one receiving *charismata* of prophecy or interpretation of tongues (viewing each instance as God's gift) but instead speaks of God giving the *charisma* of interpretation of tongues (12:10 – an expression denoting a regular ministry of this, rather than a specific instance: *cf.* 1 Cor. 14:28 *diermeneutes)*; even of God giving 'prophets' (*e.g.* Eph. 4:11 *cf.* 1 Cor. 12:28f.).
Charisma can denote the instance, or sum up a series of instances of the same enabling. But similarly, Paul expects that a man might have the gift of more than one gift – if one may put it that way. He expects the one with tongues to pray for the gift to interpret his tongues (1 Cor. 14:13). Paul recognizes pastors, evangelists, teachers, and administrators as God's gifts to the church (1 Cor. 12; Rom. 12; Eph. 4). Whether viewed as functionaries or as functions each 'gift' itself comprises *a whole nexus of charismata* (the teacher needs understanding of scripture and tradition, personal insight into his congregation, power of *paraklesis* (*cf.* Rom. 12:8) *etc.*; Paul's apostolate is God's working (Gal. 2:8), and God's grace (Rom. 1:5; 15:15) yet it seems to *include* the charismata of wonders, healing, tongues, prophecy and teaching *etc.).* Whatever God enables a man to do for the church is at the same time his gifts (severally) and his gift (viewing the separate instances of gracious enabling constatively), or better, the result of *charis* given him.

(c) Fixed Gifts?

1 Corinthians 12 emphasizes that *God* has apportioned the *charismata* (6-11, 18, 28f.) and that there is consequently no room for boasting, jealousy of inferiority (vv. 12-30). Many commentators therefore portray Paul as a fatalist in respect of the distribution of gifts. Grudem,[72] probably rightly, sees Paul as countering such an attitude in verse

---

72. Grudem, *Gifts*, pp.54-7, pp. 259-61.

31 – 'Eagerly desire the greater gifts.'[73] (cf. 14:1, 39). God's wise distribution is his choice – and not all will receive the same gift – but his choice is not independent of man's humble prayerful *seeking*. The sovereignty of the giver does not negate human responsibility.[74] Some, overimpressed by Paul's statements of divine sovereignty in the passage, have claimed for *zeloun* its classical meaning 'to practise zealously' rather than 'to seek'.[75] This does not really circumvent what they perceive to be the difficulty; for Paul, as we have seen, definitely advises in 14:13 that the one who speaks in tongues should pray to be enabled to interpret *too*. Further, it seems most natural to interpret *zeloun* semantically (in 14:1) as something like 'seek', for it is qualified 'especially that you might prophesy'.

(d) Spiritual Gifts and Natural Abilities
For Paul, as for the Old Testament, God is sovereign in the world, and that means that all that he enables are his 'gifts' among men (*cf.* 1 Cor. 7:7), though the apostle would probably not characterize them as *spiritual* as such outside the church. For Paul only Christians receive the Spirit – for reception of the Spirit is an eschatological and christocentric experience of God in Spirit that will be consummated to the individual at the parousia.[76] And it is in this context alone, of Christian reception of the Spirit, that Paul speaks of *pneumatike, charismata, domata etc.*

When Paul includes apostleship, teaching, pastoralia, administration and varieties of service in his listing of *charismata* it is obvious that the question of the relation-

---

73. The hortatory character of the passage and the parallel with 14:1 demands *zeloute* be imperative, not indicative; so Grudem, *Gift*, 56.
74. Hemphill, *Pauline Concept of Charisma*, p.124.
75. *E.g.* Van Unnik (according to Hemphill, *Ibid.*, p. 123) and T. R. Edgar, *Miraculous Gifts*, New Jersey, 1983, p. 319ff.
76. *Cf.* M. M. B. Turner, 'The Significance of Spirit-Endowment for Paul' *Vox Ev.* 9, 1975, pp. 56-69.

ship of natural abilities to spiritual gifts becomes relevant. For all Paul has to say in 1 Corinthians 2:11-13, it is clear that many of the fundamental structures of his teaching only awaited christocentric focusing, re-organization and crystallization in the Damascus Road epiphany to become his apostolic teaching[77] – and for which of his rhetorical and communication skills did he not serve at least some measure of apprenticeship in Judaism? Ultimately Paul's language of *charisma* is neutral with respect to the question of the part played by 'natural ability' – which is only proper for one who can say 'God . . . set me apart from the womb' (Gal. 1:15).

II. THE SIGNIFICANCE OF THE GIFTS FOR TODAY

In this section we must consider the following issues: 1) whether the NT assumes, either explicitly or even implicitly, that spiritual gifts would cease, 2) did any of the gifts in fact cease, and if so, what are the theological consequences? 3) the relationship between the gift of prophecy discussed in the NT and that exhibited in Charismatic circles, 4) whether the Charismatics' experience of spiritual gifts is unique, 5) whether the reception of charismatic gifts is dependent on a post-conversion crisis experience, and 6) the relationship between revelatory phenomena and theology, both yesterday and today.

1. Expected Continuation or Cessation of Gifts from the New Testament Perspective.

1 Corinthians 13 and the Pauline Evidence.
From what we have said concerning Luke's understanding of the gift of the Spirit to Christians as the gift of the Spirit of prophecy, it should be clear he envisaged the continua-

---

77. So, forcefully, Beker, *Paul* and Kim, *Origin*.

PROPHECY AND SPIRITUAL GIFTS

tion of the kinds of *charismata* to which it afforded expression.

Paul, however, explicitly states that prophecy, tongues and knowledge will cease or be done away with (1 Cor. 13:8ff.). The reason they will cease is that they are 'partial' (*ek merous*), and when 'the perfect' (*to teleion*) comes they will be superfluous (vv. 9-10). Three interpretations of what Paul means have become widely current.

i. By *to teleion* Paul denotes *the completed canon of scripture*. This is exegetically indefensible, and is not held in serious New Testament scholarship. There is no evidence that Paul expected the formation of a canon after the death of the apostles; indeed he half expected that he *might* survive to the parousia (1 Thess. 4:15f.; 1 Cor. 15:51), though he was not sure. The Corinthians could hardly be expected to perceive from the phrase *to teleion* that he was referring to a canon of scripture, and even if they could, the completed canon of scripture would hardly signify for the Corinthians the *passing away of merely 'partial' knowledge* (and prophecy and tongues with it), and the arrival of 'full knowledge', for the Corinthians already had the Old Testament, the Gospel Tradition (presumably), and more Pauline teaching than finally got into the canon (certainly)! But the most compelling reason is that in verse 12b Paul states that (with the coming of 'the perfect') our 'partial knowledge' will give way to a measure of knowledge that is matched only by the way we *are* now *known (by God)*.[78] This contrast between Corinthian knowledge before and after the arrival of *to teleion* is so sharp that Paul can express it 'Now we see but a poor reflection; then we shall see face to face' (v. 12a, NIV). The use of the language of theophany,[79] makes it all but certain that Paul is talking of the parousia.

---

78. G. Bornkamm, *Early Christian Experience*, London, 1969, p. 185.
79. Grudem, *Gift,* p. 213, n. 57.

However much we respect the New Testament canon, Paul can only be accused of the wildest exaggeration in verse 12 if *that* is what he was talking about.

ii. That *to teleion* means 'maturity'. Lexically this is possible (the illustration in v. 11 is often taken to confirm it), but to suggest that this may apply to some pre-parousia maturity of the church merely trivializes the language of verses 10 and 12. Besides which we must note (1) that Paul so highly ranks prophets and prophecy that it is unlikely he would envisage them excluded from even the most mature church (*cf.* 1 Cor. 14:37) and (2) Paul in 1 Corinthians 1:7 clearly regards the charismata as strengthening the church as it awaits the Lord's return.

iii. The eschatological interpretation. Only this interpretation satisfactorily accounts for Paul's language in verses 8-12. The point in verse 11 is that the whole existence of the church on earth is characterized by partial knowledge (prophecy *etc.*) when seen from the perspective of the coming parousia, not that the apostolic church will give rise to a more mature one *on earth*, in which knowledge will no longer be *ek merous*. The corollary is that Paul *expects* prophecy, 'knowledge' and (possibly) tongues to continue (note the adversative *de* of v. 10); it is *only* the advent of the parousia, and the conditions it introduces, that makes prophecy otiose (*cf. katargethesetai* vv. 8, 10); not some unspecified event or condition before it.

2. Did any of the Gifts in Fact Cease, and if so, What are the Theological Consequences?

It is not possible to answer the question whether any of the gifts ceased. Claims to various of them were made in the post-Apostolic church and thereafter, but nevertheless *relatively sparsely*; from this we may infer that they were at least much less prominent in the later church than at the beginning and that a wide range of cultural, sociological and theological factors may have been at play in the shaping of the expectation, and consequent distribution, of gifts in the church.

What theological significance would such an observation carry? The outright (Reformed?) claim that all 'spectacular gifts' ceased with the immediate apostolic circle would require a sharp end of all such Christian claims by Justin's day. And a number of dispensationalists have attempted to read the patristic evidence in just that way, at some cost to their claim to objectivity.[80] The sharp line is not there; nor anywhere else. And, anyway, the New Testament itself does not encourage the view that these gifts were *merely* 'signs', or provisional substitutes for the canon.

What can be claimed with some confidence is that such gifts were marginalized. The factors concerned were probably very complex. Prophecy may well have become increasingly peripheral, as Aune suggests, (1) because Christian doctrine, tradition and norms were gradually established and fell within the province of teachers and pastors to administer, and (2) as, sociologically, the church became more integrated with its environment, and less prone to the dynamics of a millenarian sect. As for incomprehensible 'tongues', they had little built-in survival value, and it is hardly surprising that they mainly fell out of view until they were made the hall-mark of Spirit-baptism in early Pentecostalism, and until later culturally and existentially orientated factors could undergird them in Charismatic circles. Healing of the body soon came to be detached from the gospel proper, by platonizing of the latter, and so became eclipsed, only to re-emerge in the church with an entirely different theological significance.

---

80. See the criticisms in Hunter, 'Tongues Speech: A Patristic Analysis' *JETS* 23, 1980, *passim*.

3. What Relationship Exists Between the Gift of Prophecy Discussed in the New Testament and That Exhibited in Charismatic Circles?

By 'prophecy', it will be remembered, we do not mean to denote expository preaching (see *e.g.* Best, Grudem and Hill), nor even charismatic exegesis (*contra* Hill), but Christian oracular speech; the rendering of a message considered by a Christian to have been imparted to him directly by the Spirit in a 'word' or 'vision'. From examples heard, directly or on tape, and from popular literature, my impression is that modern prophecy roughly coheres with the New Testament pattern at the following points:

i. The understanding of prophecy is that it is oracular speech based on a perceptible revelatory event or impulse – this is usually marked by some standard formula such as 'The Lord says . . . ' or the like, followed either by direct or indirect speech understood as expressing the content of the oracle; or by a description of a visionary phenomenon.

ii. The condition of the prophet varies from that of mild dissociation to (controlled) trance state; usually somewhere nearer the former.

iii. The *content* of prophetic pronouncements is very rarely if ever primarily doctrinal; rather, it is parallel to oracles of assurance, prescriptive oracles, oracles of judgement (rare) or of salvation, legitimation oracles and personalized predictive oracles (rare) – *i.e.* the sort we have noted in the New Testament. In other words, modern Charismatic prophecy seems to operate chiefly within the area which is not directly the focus of scripture, and where specific knowledge or guidance may be required.

iv. Prophetic oracles share the same mixed and enigmatic quality of authority evinced in 1 Corinthians 14 and 1 Thessalonians 5. They are *not* to my knowledge treated at the same level of authority as scripture, but sometimes even passed over quite rapidly and without comment if the congregation evaluates them as lacking in charismatic authority. More striking oracular speech usually provokes actual response by way of discussion or leadership comment, which in turn is guided, where relevant, by scripture and tradition. If, then, the prophecy is prescriptive (or if diagnostic, but implying required action) the church may decide that the oracle is binding on it – but only in the way more traditional churches might feel 'led' to some specific decision by God, and so adopt it. Some churches may (accidentally) have marginalized biblical exposition in their zeal for the prophetic word for today, but I have no reliable account of any congregation actually formally accepting a proposition to the effect that charismatic authority stands on a par with scripture, far less above it. Almost invariably, scripture is given absolute authority – at least in theory – while prophetic words are accorded only relative, albeit sometimes substantial, authority. Even in those movements which claim 'apostles', the title is not used to imply that their prophetic speech is to be regarded as carrying canonical status.

v. Modern prophecy is especially seen to fulfil the role expressed in 1 Corinthians 14:3 of encouragement, strengthening and exhortation of the church.[81]

Moving to points of difference, we might note:

i. Except for somewhat stereotyped openings and (more rarely) endings, modern oracular speech is *relatively* lacking in distinctive prophetic forms[82] (though archaizing

81. Hill, *NT Prophecy* 210 (following Hollenweger) believes Pentecostal prophecy is dominated by exhortation; Poloma, *Charismatic Movement* 57 finds this unusual in Pentecostal circles but more characteristic of neo-Pentecostal gatherings.
82. The examples cited by Poloma, *ibid.*, 58, however, have clear form.

language is commonplace). This difference may be more apparent than real for (a) it is precisely the well-formed oracles embedded in the early literature that tend to be 'rediscovered'; (b) in the New Testament there is already a tendency to mixture of Old Testament forms, and to the formless (so Aune);[83] (c) there is evidence that some oracular speech in the New Testament period consisted not merely of declaration of revelation, but that this was mixed with response by the prophet (*e.g.* Acts 21:4). If revelation were declared in *indirect* speech and integrated with response, typical oracular speech-forms would be lost.

ii. Another difference lies in the fact that *some* modern 'prophecy' does not rest on *previous reception* of the word of the Lord by the individual, but is regarded as a simultaneous reception and transmission of the oracle or vision. Where the Old Testament prophet said 'I saw ... ', the modern prophet more often says 'I see ... '[84] Stephen's speech in Acts 7:55f., is an example of this,[85] but it does not seem to have been the norm – and the practice today is a slightly dangerous one, eliminating the possibility of prior evaluation of a 'word' before it is given out.[86]

These differences, however, do not appear to be material, and New Testament prophetic speech seems functionally and formally to resemble the modern phenomenon of the same name. Prophecy today cannot, however, expect to play the same *foundational* role as it did in the earliest period (*cf.* Eph. 2:20 *etc.*) for the reasons mentioned above and to be discussed further below.

---

83. Aune, *Prophecy,* chap. 10.
84. Not exclusively, see Poloma, *Charismatic Movement* 59.
85. On this phenomenon, see Aune, *Prophecy* pp.148-51.
86. See the warning by Grudem, *Gift,* p. 261.

PROPHECY AND SPIRITUAL GIFTS

4. Is the Charismatics' Experience Unique?

With respect to the gifts of prophesy, tongues and healings, we are compelled to answer 'No'.[87] There are historical parallels to 'tongues' in the church; claims to healing can be found outside the Charismatic tradition and independent of it (*e.g.* in 'the Guild of Health' and 'the Guild of St Raphael' in Anglicanism; the Iona Community *etc.*); [88] and prophecy too, when rightly understood (*i.e.* when it is not generalized to the point where it merely connotes phenomena related to prophetism such as God-enabled preaching, teaching, or 'any verbal enforcement of biblical teaching as it applies to one's present hearers'[89]), is located in many if not all streams of evangelicalism. The phenomenon of oracular speech itself, in some forms, *is* being exercised in evangelical circles, albeit not given the name 'prophecy'. Most spiritually-minded evangelicals seek God's guidance on decisions which they know the Bible cannot settle for them; and many expect that God will sometimes give them a definite and direct indication – a 'word from the Lord' on the matter. Where such is experienced, and related to others *to whom it is also directed*,[90] we have the dynamics of what the New Testament means by 'prophecy', and of what is experienced in Charismatic circles and labelled 'prophecy' there.

There are *differentia* of *form*: the evangelical tends to say, 'The Lord laid on my heart last night . . . ' or 'The Lord told me . . . ' and *invariably* proceeds to *indirect* speech

87. See Paker's telling criticism, *Keep in Step*, p. 197ff, and *passim*.
88. See M. Kelsey, *Healing and Christianity*, London, 1973, chap. 9.
89. Packer, *Keep in Step,* p. 215.
90. It seems pointless to use the term 'prophecy' as such to denote 'messages' which are primarily, or exclusively, intended for the one to whom the revelation comes. That this is a gift with identical dynamics, however, need not be doubted. For Judaism such an operation would certainly be a function of the 'Spirit of prophecy'; *cf.,* Targ. Ps. Jonathan Ex 33:16; Gen R 75.8; Tanh (Buber) 'Vayesh'.

where the Charismatic often prefers *direct* speech.[91] there are also *differentia* of *frequency* and of *range of content* (Charismatics tend to have greater expectation here, and do not merely approach God for 'solicited oracles' in answer to specific questions) and of *power of delivery* (some Charismatics become skilled practitioners) – but the evangelical experiences cannot be sharply divided off from the Charismatic; they too lie within the boundaries of the ancient patterns of oracular speech. As to the clarity of perception of the initial revelatory experience, there are, among those I have questioned, no necessary differences between the two groups: some evangelicals claim (occasionally) remarkably strong and clear 'words' (rarely, however, visionary leading) on an issue; many Charismatics would confess very indistinct 'reception' of some prophecies.

The biggest dividing line within these phenomena lies not across the evangelical/Charismatic border, but *within* Charismatic circles – it is the line between those who open their mouths and speak out a 'prophecy' without any idea of what is coming (for which there is no actual New Testament basis) and those who at least have some notion of the message before they speak at all (in accord with the New Testament).[92] If evangelicals hesitate to use the term 'prophecy' to denote the sort of phenomenon we have described, it is perhaps due to a mistaken understanding of New Testament prophecy, namely as a primarily doctrinal revelation parallel in authority to canonical prophecy. Here Grudem's thesis may serve to tumble the barriers between the two groups.

91. We say 'prefers' intentionally, for the 'prophet' can choose whether to speak in archaizing English or modern English; whether in direct speech or indirect speech; *cf.*, B. Yocum, *Prophecy: Exercising the Prophetic Gifts of the Spirit in the Church Today*, Ann Arbor, 1976, p. 82ff.
92. See Yocum, *ibid*, 75ff: sometimes at least the first words of a 'message' are received, p. 78f.

When we say the Charismatic experience is not unique, but found in other churches, to some degree, we do not of course imply that it is found in those churches in biblical or ideal measure. If Charismatic churches are in danger of overemphasizing some gifts in relation to others, it may well be that evangelical churches have marginalized and underemphasized them.

5. Is There any Reason to Assume that Reception of Charismatic Gifts Depends on a Post-Conversion Crisis Experience?

Given what we have argued earlier – that there is no Pauline basis for restricting charismata to a special, 'Spirit-baptized' group and that the gift of the Spirit in Acts 2 is no *donum superadditum* of power – the advent of what Luke might call the Spirit of prophecy does not create a special class of spiritually gifted Christians over against others. Rather, it brings to *each* the means of receiving not only 'communion with the Lord' viewed generally, but also the same concretely specified in charismata of heavenly wisdom and knowledge. These may then inform the teacher, guide the missionary, lead in individual decisions, give diagnosis to the pastor, 'irresistible wisdom' and power to the preacher, or be related as prophecy to the congregation or other individuals. The 'power' received by the apostles (*cf.* Acts 1:8) was not something *in addition* to Joel's promised gift, but precisely *an intense experience of* some of the charismata which are part and parcel of the operation of the Spirit as Joel's promised Spirit of prophecy.

Far from indicating some new post-conversion Spirit-baptism (a whole concept which rests on a misunderstanding of Luke's terminology),[93] tongues and prophecy,

---

93. The phrase, 'baptize in (the) (Holy) Spirit (and fire)' in the NT is found on the lips of John the Baptist, Jesus (Acts 1:56) and Peter (Acts 11:16) and, perhaps, in the writings of Paul (1 Cor.

where they are initially expressed (Acts 2:4; 10:46; 19:6), *appropriately signal* the advent of the Spirit *qua* the Spirit of prophecy described above. The reception of this gift initiates and enables that relationship to the heavenly Lord which both marks true Christian existence and which readily comes to expression in the various charismata of prophetism noted above.

Not surprisingly many scholars in the Charismatic movement have tended to concede that post-ascension reception of the Spirit in Paul and Luke marks the beginning of Christian life, not a second level. Some have even recognized that the language of being 'filled by' the Spirit cannot successfully be correlated with a second-blessing theology.[94] There has consequently been a tendency, especially in Catholic Charismatic circles, to differentiate between theological and *objective* Spirit baptism/reception, tied to initiation, and *subjective* experience of the same, introducing people to the world of charismata.[95] Since there is no separate theoretical, biblical basis for this, this position really seems to be a theologizing of the following (flawed) practical argument.

The argument runs: *in practice* Christians receive empowering and charismatic gifts only *after* some initiating, and consciously realized, spiritual crisis experience labelled 'Spirit-baptism' (usually, but not always associated with speaking in tongues). It rests on a misunderstanding in that it presupposes (and perpetuates!) experiential dualisms and absolutizes one of them, thereby suggesting that 'Pentecostal' experience is fundamentally different in

---

12:13), it is only just beginning to be realized - *cf.*, C. E. Hummel, *Fire in the Fireplace*, London, 1979, chap. 14 - that these usages are not uniform but amount to different metaphors, topic *and* illustration being subtly different in each case.
94. See Turner, 'Spirit Endowment', pp. 53-55.
95. *Cf.* Hummel, *Fireplace*, p. 171; T. Smail, *Reflected Glory: The Spirit in Christ and Christians*, London, 1975, chaps. 6, 10; L. J. Suenens, *A New Pentecost?*, London, 1975, p. 80f.

kind – in a different, supernatural, realm – from evangelical experience.

Of those who claim to fit the pattern there seem to me to be at least three types: (i) A few, styling themselves 'Spirit-baptized', who have had an intense crisis-experience of the Spirit with vigorous manifestations. Testimonies to this are not lacking.[96] (ii) A much larger group who, having had a *subjectively* strong, but not especially vigorously manifested experience, probably spontaneously spoke in tongues and may even have been 'slain in the Spirit', or the like. (iii) Again a large group, who, when prayed for, had no *spontaneous* experience (other than mild euphoria), but were persuaded to initiate tongues speech, and, on achieving this, accepted (by faith) that they had received the same package as types (i) and (ii) – though they may even register disappointment concerning their experience if pressed.

All types usually discover changes in their pattern of spirituality after the crisis experience, perhaps most marked in type (i), but not necessarily so. There are usually claims to greater awareness of the Lord, deepened and more expectant faith, greater joy, and development of a new range of charismata. *But* this tends to lead to preaching and teaching of an exaggerated experiential dualism (much, or all, was sin, doubt and weakness before; much, or all, is faith, power and victory now); and where such teaching is accepted it is liable to become self-fulfilling creating a negative expectation in people with respect to the possibility of 'gifts' before their own 'crisis-experience', and a positive one afterwards.

Worse still, such exaggerated personal experiential dualism tends to be projected on to the Charismatic/evangelical divide to create a claimed experiential dualism between relatively powerless evangelicals,

---

96. *Cf.* the composite 'testimony' in J. P. Kildahl, 'Psychological Observations' in M. P. Hamilton (ed), *The Charismatic Movement*, Grand Rapids, 1975, p. 125.

lacking charismata, and Charismatics living in victory, power and the plenitude of charismata. It is this last dualism which popularly undergirds the 'practical argument' for pursuing a post-conversion 'Spirit-baptism'.

Unfortunately for the practical argument the dualism breaks down when examined. Healing is not a gift confined to 'Charismatics', even if practised more often by them. Similarly, as we have seen, 'words of the Lord' or 'revelations' (in the general New Testament sense) are not given to neo-Pentecostalists alone but are widely reported (albeit in different language) in the evangelical literature too. In other words, on closer examination there is no sharp dividing line between evangelical experience and the neo-Pentecostalist one. There is no question of leaving a *charismaless* Christianity for a charismatic one. The basic difference is one of degree and not of kind; one of emphasis, and not absolute. Being forced to accept that one stands on the wrong side of an experiential dualism, and so to seek 'Spirit-baptism' as the gateway to greener pastures, may be *one* way of passing from the evangelical pole to the Charismatic. But it is neither a necessary way, nor an appropriate way, for the very reason that it suggests passage from one *kind* of Christian experience to another of a *different kind.*

If the evangelical Christian wishes to become a 'Charismatic' (the more common route), what he should need is not laying on of hands and a crisis-experience, but merely the sort of teaching given in 'Charismatic' circles to the 'freshly Spirit-baptized' (who are considered *by virtue of having been Spirit-baptized* to have the potential of any of the gifts, needing only to learn how to discern and use them). Our counter-thesis is simply that it is *not* by virtue of some second 'Spirit-baptism'. but by initially receiving the Spirit as Luke's promised Spirit of prophecy, that *any* Christian has such potential.

6. What is the Relation Between Revelatory Experiences and Theology, Yesterday and Today?

Many evangelicals fear that the emphasis of the 'Charismatic movement' on revelatory phenomena implies the dangerous possibility of new authoritative revelation. That is, however, a red herring. The gifts Paul mentions in 1 Corinthians 12:8-10 he expected to be widespread in the churches; the determination of the gospel, by contrast, he regarded as an *apostolic* function (Gal. 1-2 *etc.*). *This* revelation provides the test of the revelatory charismata, not *vice versa*. Hence Paul's clear subordination of the authority of the prophetic phenomena at Corinth to his own (*cf.* 14:37ff.). Not feeling able to allow the Corinthian prophets to decide the agenda for worship, he specified *how* they were to operate, and further relativised their authority by demanding congregational sifting of their utterances.

Today we would be surprised and alarmed if anyone outside of sectarian movements tried to add to or tamper with the fundamental structures of theology in the name of some revelatory experience. But within the broad framework of 'established' theology, there is still a need for the illumination of and the application to twentieth-century situations of gospel truth and apostolic praxis. There is a need, too, for deep spiritual diagnosis of individuals and congregations, and of specific leading on a host of practical issues. *These* are the areas in which the revelatory gifts of 1 Corinthians 12:8-10 have contemporary relevance.

Although today's wise pastor, leader or interpreter has infinitely more by way of aid through the precedents and norms laid down in centuries of church history and reflection, ultimately it is still only by the Spirit's work that God gives shape to his church and directs its growth. In the light of our discussion in this paper, we can say that the Spirit's sovereign work in the man of God is evidenced in two ways: (1) without him necessarily being conscious of the Spirit (*cf.* 1 Cor. 2:6) and (2) where he is *immediately perceived* as giving direction. Today's pastor or leader is in as much need as ever of such immediate charismata of wisdom, direction and heavenly knowledge. Where evangelicals seek the Lord this way, the difference between them and 'Charismatics' on the issue of the relation of theology and revelatory events is minimalized.

Ultimately, the issue raised by the so-called 'Charismatic movement' is not so much a theoretical one as a practical one. It concerns how we find the right balance between the Spirit's sovereignly creative work in our disciplined and prayerful study of scripture, and the Spirit's more immediately perceived leading.

LUTHER'S QUARREL WITH THE *SCHWÄRMER*

DAVID F. WRIGHT

It is not surprising that Lutheran assessments of the contemporary movement of charismatic renewal often refer to Luther's critique of what he called *Schwärmerei*. This German word is difficult to translate satisfactorily into English. It is normally rendered as 'enthusiasm' or 'fanaticism'. Those who displayed this spirit in their religion were labelled the *Schwärmer* (which in German can be either singular or plural). We will shortly look more closely at what the term may have implied for Luther. Those whom he so characterized have seemed to some modern Lutheran bodies not unlike the charismatic Christians of the later twentieth century.

'A Pastoral Perspective' on the charismatic movement adopted by the Lutheran Church in America in 1974 declared:

> Lutheran charismatics should resist any understanding of the Spirit's indwelling which de-emphasises or renders superfluous the proclamation of the Word, the sacraments, or the Christian fellowship. A narrow concept of the activity of the Holy Spirit is unacceptable and open to all Luther's criticism on the Enthusiasts.[1]

---

1. *Presence Power Praise. Documents on the Charismatic Renewal*, 3 vols. ed. Kilian McDonnell, Collegeville, Minn., 1980, vol.1, p. 564 (cited hereafter as McDonnell). This paper was written before I had seen Carter Lindberg's study, *The Third Reformation? Charismatic Movements and the Lutheran Tradition* (Macon, Georgia, 1983). Lindberg concentrates on Luther's response to five major 'spiritualists', Carlstadt, Müntzer, Melchior Hofmann, Sebastian Franck and Caspar Schwenckfeld. Lindberg summarizes his position in P. Manns & H. Meyer (edd.), *Luther's Ecumenical Significance: An Interconfessional Consultation* (Philadelphia, 1984), pp. 161-181, with useful critiques by J. F. McCue (pp. 203-207), C. A. Pater (pp. 207-215) and J. S. Oyer (pp. 215-219).

A report of the Lutheran Church Missouri Synod in 1972 explained that 'Luther and the Lutheran Confessions describe as "enthusiasm" (*Schwärmerei*) the view that God reveals himself and bestows his spiritual gifts apart from the objective and external Word and sacraments'. It then cites the Schmalkaldic Articles drawn up by Luther in 1537:

> Enthusiasm clings to Adam and his descendants from the beginning to the end of the world. It is a poison implanted and inoculated in man by the old dragon, and it is the source, strength and power of all heresy, including that of the papacy and Mohammedanism.... Whatever is attributed to the Spirit apart from (the) Word and sacrament is of the devil. (3:8:9-10)[2]

Not all such Lutheran references to Luther's encounter with *Schwärmerei* have regarded it as obviously relevant to the challenge posed to the mainstream Churches by the charismatic renewal. Nor have all Lutheran Churches reached so negative an estimate of the movement as the Missouri Synod.[3]

Nevertheless, the analogy between sixteenth-century *Schwärmerei* and present-day charismatic stirrings appears to suggest itself almost instinctively to Lutherans.[4]

2. McDonnell, vol. 1, p. 352. The Articles were cited again in 1977 by the Missouri Synod in a set of guidelines for congregations and pastors (McDonnell, vol. 2, p. 313).
3. McDonnell, vol. 1, p. lvii, asserts that German Lutheranism has adopted a more positive stance, perhaps because Lutheran charismatics in Germany have placed greater stress on integration and theological reflection. The same is true of Scandinavian Lutheranism. For some reason McDonnell includes no documents from the Scandinavian churches.
4. Hardly any documents of non-Lutheran origin make the connection. The 1976 report of the Presbyterian Church in Canada on 'The Work of the Spirit' notes that 'The attitudes of Luther and Calvin toward the "enthusiasts" and "spiritualists" of their day were the initial forces shaping the outlook that Presbyterians are prone to take towards Neo-Pentecostalism', but also affirms that 'The "enthusiasts" who plagued the Reformers cannot be

LUTHER'S QUARREL WITH THE *SCHWÄRMER*

We will return later in this paper to a closer look at the parallels discerned by these Lutheran commentaries. For the most part, however, historical enquiry must occupy our attention.

Who Were Luther's *Schwärmer*?

Luther gives us, of course, no systematic answer to this question. In the Schmalkaldic Articles, as we have seen, he identified *Schwärmerei* as 'the source, strength and power of all heresy, including that of the papacy and Mohammedanism'. A modern Lutheran encyclopedia includes even Calvin among Protestant 'enthusiasts'![5] In fact, although Luther uses the designation with disconcerting freedom, if not almost indiscriminately, its primary reference seems to be to the radicalism of Carlstadt, the Zwickau Prophets and Thomas Müntzer in the early 1520s. These representatives of what is now commonly called 'the Radical Reformation' all believed that Luther's protest against corrupt Catholicism had not gone far enough or fast enough. They all stood for a more drastic reform of the Church, marked, for example, by a more stringent biblicism in sacramental practice and by the removal of the divide between laity and clergy. Spiritual experience was strongly emphasised, in the form of both visions or dreams, which were cited as divine authentication of their message, and an essential religious inwardness enjoyed by all true Christians.

By natural extension the label is applied by Luther to the rebellious peasants of the mid-1520s, whom Müntzer led into battle, and in the latter part of the decade to the Anabaptists. In the same years it also embraces Luther's mainstream Reformation opponents in the 'Supper-strife',

---

    identified with Neo-Pentecostals, and we may not simply apply to the latter the complaints of the Reformers against the former' (McDonnell, vol. 2, pp. 241, 245).
5. G. Krodel, s.v. 'Enthusiasm', in *The Encyclopedia of the Lutheran Church*, ed. J. Bodensieck, Minneapolis, 1963, vol. 1, pp. 783-788, at p. 787.

chiefly Zwingli and Oecolampadius, the Reformers respectively of Zürich and Basel, but also Martin Bucer of Strasbourg. The Lord's Supper was the storm-centre of the first serious disagreement between the leaders of the Reformation. Most of the Reformers of Switzerland and South Germany rejected Luther's understanding of the manner of Christ's presence in the Supper. They inclined in various ways to more metaphorical or symbolic or 'spiritual' interpretations of the Words of Institution. The often bitter dispute deeply damaged the Protestant movement, with Luther vigorously attacking as *Schwärmer* those who evaded the plain sense of 'This (bread) *is* my body'. Later still, the alleged 'antinomianism' of his former colleague at Wittenberg, Johann Agricola, was tarred by Luther with the same brush of *Schwärmerei*.

Whatever the injustice to our minds of encompassing so wide a span, for example, Müntzer and Bucer, within a single characterization, Luther would often point to direct influences, such as that of Carlstadt's eucharistic tracts upon the Zürich or Strasbourg sacramentarians (as Luther's opponents in the Supper-strife were called), or prominent similarities, like that between the rejection of infant baptism without the advocacy of believers' baptism by Nicholas Storch, one of the Zwickau Prophets, and the practice of the Anabaptists proper.[6]

6. The range of Luther's concept of *Schwarmerei* is stressed by Krodel (see previous note); J. S. Oyer, *Lutheran Reformers Against Anabaptists. Luther, Melanchthon and Menius and the Anabaptists of Central Germany*, The Hague, 1964; and Mark U. Edwards, Jr., 'Seurmerus. Luther's Own Fanatics', in *Seven-Headed Luther. Essays in Commemoration of a Quincentenary 1483-1983*, ed. P. N. Brooks, Oxford, 1983, pp. 123-146. Edwards omits the Anabaptists, because Luther was never involved in a major controversy with them (*Luther and the False Brethren*, Stanford, 1975, p. 209 n. 4). Oyer's concern is to show that the deep suspiciousness engendered in Luther by the early *Schwärmer* (Carlstadt, the Zwickau Prophets, Müntzer) not only biased him against the Anabaptists but also blinded him to such an obvious feature as their biblical literalism, or perhaps

LUTHER'S QUARREL WITH THE *SCHWÄRMER*

More fundamentally, Luther believed that all his critics who demanded in varying degrees more radical reform were the mouthpieces of a single foe - the devil. His conviction of their Satanic inspiration finds wearisome expression in his writings.[7] Furthermore, by discerning his opponents' unity in discord and ascribing it to the devil, Luther could think, speak and write as badly of the best of them as of the worst. If Müntzer as the agent of Satan had become a rabble-rouser and a rebel, so too could leaders of urban reform like Zwingli, Oecolampadius and Bucer, who were fired by the same 'spirit'. Hence, at the conclusion of one of his major contributions to the eucharistic controversy, Luther warns the city fathers of Basel and Strasbourg to beware: 'Müntzer is dead, but his spirit is not yet eradicated'.[8] In his works against the sacramentarian views of the Swiss, he regularly conjures up the ghosts of Carlstadt and Müntzer. Since the former, respectable magisterial Reformers though they be, have the same spirit as the latter, they will bring forth the same fruit.[9] The differences between them were only superficial. Luther felt justified in attacking not so much the men themselves and what they had actually done, as their

---

rather enabled him to attack them with confidence despite his limited knowledge of them.

7. When Oecolampadius complained, Luther retorted: 'I would do well if every other word I write were "devil". Shall I now become so timid for the sake of these delicate, highly spiritual, profoundly holy fanatics, that I must avoid mentioning my enemy? ... My frank, public, simple snapping at the devil suits me better than their poisonous, sneaky stabbing, which under the guise of peace and love they practice against the upright', *Confession Concerning Christ's Supper* (1528), tr. R. H. Fischer in *Luther's Works* (edd. J. Pelikan and H. T. Lehmann, Philadelphia and St Louis, 1958ff. - 'American edition', hereafter *LW*), 37: 270. *D. Martin Luthers Werke. Kritische Gesamtausgabe* (Weimar, 1883ff., hereafter *WA*) 26: 402.
8. *That These Words of Christ 'This is My Body', etc., Still Stand Firm Against the Fanatics* (1527), tr. Fischer, *LW* 37: 150; *WA* 23:283.
9. *Ibid., LW* 37: 137; *WA* 23: 263.

'spirit' and what they were capable of doing.[10] How confidently he anticipated Müntzerite sedition and bloodshed from Zwingli and Bucer we can perhaps not gauge. But he clearly expected civil disorder to ensue from the unauthorised, clandestine preaching of the Anabaptists, and ended up directly accusing them of Müntzerite revolutionary views.[11]

The Satanic motivation of those who propounded teachings that conflicted with his own led Luther to doubt their orthodoxy in other articles of faith. He could accordingly 'regard Zwingli as un-Christian, with all his teaching, for he holds and teaches no part of the Christian faith rightly'.[12] Whatever such *Schwärmer* did was liable to be interpreted in the worst possible light. If they stuck to their guns and held out against argument and admonition, they were guilty of Satanic obduracy; if they professed some measure of uncertainty and a willingness to discuss other possibilities, this was proof positive of their lack of the Holy Spirit, who is 'the sort of teacher who is sure and makes men sure', imparting *'plerophoria* in Christ, a full, certain, sure understanding, upon which a man can die and risk everything'.[13] Similarly the Spirit is the Spirit of unity and cannot have anything to do with the diversity of sacramentarian opinions.[14] Carlstadt's less than pellucid

---

10. Edwards, *art.cit.*, pp. 142-143. 'It ought surprise no one that I call him a devil. For I am not thinking of Dr Carlstadt or concerned about him. I am thinking of him by whom he is possessed and for whom he speaks' (*Against the Heavenly Prophets in the Matter of Images and Sacraments*, 1525, tr. B. Erling and C. Bergendoff, *LW* 40: 149; *WA* 18: 139).
11. Oyer, *op cit.*, pp. 126-129.
12. *Confession Concerning Christ's Supper, LW* 37: 231; *WA* 26: 342.
13. *That These Words of Christ, LW* 37: 126; *WA* 23: 245. Cf. Edwards, *art.cit.*, p. 143. 'Satan needs do no more through the *Schwärmer* than always to produce doubts' (*Concerning Rebaptism. A Letter of Martin Luther to Two Pastors*, 1528, tr. C. Bergendoff, *LW* 40: 262; *WA* 26: 173).
14. *Confession* (apropos of Schwenckfeld), *LW* 37:289; *WA* 26:434.

style betrays him, for 'the Holy Spirit speaks well, clearly, in an orderly and distinct fashion. Satan mumbles and chews the words in his mouth.'[15] The insecurities and anxieties of his opponents' writings, when they beg for peace or crave instruction or shy away from causing offence, illustrate for Luther the prophetic judgment on the wicked who have no rest (Isaiah 57:20). 'A sure conscience which is certain about the matter, does not hem and haw so.'[16]

The bitterness of the Supper-strife among the first generation of Protestants often amazes and dismays modern Christians. Its acrid tones demonstrate how fateful were Luther's earlier clashes with Carlstadt, the Zwickau Prophets and Müntzer, from which was largely constructed that image of the *Schwärmer* with which he later identified other opponents, especially those he once lumped together as 'the sacramentarian and baptist fanatics'.[17] For such a variety of targets, *Schwärmer* cannot be a descriptive term.[18] The basic meaning of *'Schwärm'* in German is 'swarm' (of bees, birds, etc.). Figuratively it denotes a 'craze' or 'mania'. (In modern German 'für die Bühne schwärmen' is 'to be stagestruck'; 'to be crazy about someone, to have a crush on someone' is 'für jemanden schwärmen'.) Luther's *Schwärmer* is a pejorative label, better translated 'fanatic' rather than 'enthusiast'. 'Enthusiasm', in the sense in which this word has been used in the study of religion, no doubt well describes important aspects of some of Luther's *Schwärmer* (e.g., the

15. *Against the Heavenly Prophets, LW* 40: 118; *WA* 18: 101-102.
16. *That These Words of Christ, LW 37*: 29-30; *WA* 23: 89.
17. *Confession, LW* 37: 360; *WA* 26: 499.
18. Luther's use of the word is rarely analyzed linguistically. It is included in the series of derogatory names used for the Anabaptists by contemporaries, around which Leonard Verduin constructs *The Reformers and their Stepchildren* (Grand Rapids, 1964), but only in the composite form 'Sacramentschwärmer'. For an extraordinary modern misuse of the latinised *Suvermerus*, see C. Hopf, *Martin Bucer and the English Reformation* (Oxford, 1946), pp. 35-40.

claim to enjoy immediate contact with God without external means), but the German term itself does not so much embody his analysis of their religion as purvey his judgment on their disordered and excited extremist. Luther's usage is probably based more on the figurative than the literal sense of *Schwärmer*, without losing sight of the latter. Like birds of the air, his *Schwärmer* lost touch with the ground, with bedrock reality. In their excitement they were walking on air. Or perhaps like bees they gave the impression of frantically busy activity to little apparent effect.

Unifying Principles?

If, then, Luther's *Schwärmer* were so heterogeneous, did not basic features of their dissent justify their categorization by this single term? Do no consistent fundamental convictions or attributes lie concealed behind their patent diversity? Gerhard Krodel identified two root causes of *Schwärmerei* - the fusion of the 'two kingdoms' which Luther sharply distinguished, together with a corresponding confusion between law and gospel, and secondly, the disjunction of Spirit from Word, of inward from outward, separating what Luther always conjoined.[19] This paper will concentrate on the latter, partly because it is in this area that Luther's conflict with *Schwärmerei* is most obviously relevant to those questions about experience of the Spirit thrown up by the charismatic movement, and partly because Luther's encounters with *Schwärmer* of various kinds clearly focus more commonly on the second than on the first of Krodel's two basic errors of *Schwärmerei*. This is not to deny that failure to distinguish between the two kingdoms or between law and gospel is prominent enough in Luther's attacks on *Schwärmer*. The Zwickau Prophets' radical critique of the socio-economic order sided with the simple folk and took a stand against the harshness of rulers and the pride of riches. In Thomas Müntzer's revo-

19. *Art.cit.* (n. 5 above).

lutionary spiritualism, in the rebellion of the peasants and in the millenarian violence of Münster, Luther was horrified at the overthrow of civil authority in the name of religion. He feared too that Carlstadt's iconoclasm was a stage on the road to revolution, and indeed, as we have seen, he suspected all *Schwärmer* of threatening to break out into riot and tumult. Furthermore, his theological charge against Carlstadt accused him of imposing a new kind of legalism, while it was for antinomianism that Agricola was cast as a *Schwärmer* by Luther.

In reality, the false disjunction of inward and outward is in Luther's thought closely related to the refusal to recognize the authority of rulers. The function of civil government was no less appointed by God than the ministerial office of Word and sacrament. For Luther the Church's ministry, the family and the state were the three main *Stände* established by God for the ordering of the life of sinful mankind. 'Order' or 'structure' might be the best English equivalent of Luther's *Stand*. Luther explicitly equated the *Schwärmer's* rejection of civil government with their disdain for material instruments of God's Word. To the *Schwärmer* both were externals and hence of no avail. The democratic spirit was a spirit of *Schwärmerei*, for it sought to bypass God's appointed agent - the prince or emperor, and gain direct, unmediated access to God's authority in human society. More than one nuance can be detected in Luther's dictum, 'He who rejects baptism rejects the emperor'.[20]

Disorder and the Appeal to the Masses
There runs through Luther's reforming career a dread of popular tumult, amounting at times almost to paranoia.

20. See the essay 'Stand and Sakrament' in H. J. Iwand, *Glaubensgerechtigkeit. Gesammelte Aufsätze* II, ed. G. Sauter (*Theol. Bücherei System. Theol.* 64; Munich, 1980), and the same author's *Luther's Theologie*, ed. J. Haar (*Nachgelassene Werke*, edd. H. Gollwitzer *et al.*, vol. 5; Munich, 1974), pp. 290-308.

The maintenance of the stability of society was always of prime importance. He was as alert to any threat to subvert governmental authority by appeal to the populace at large as he was insistent upon steadfast adherence to one's ordered 'station' and calling in the community. In different ways the *Schwärmer* spirit imperilled such good order.

In one of his most important statements on the relation between inward (Spirit) and outward (Word), Luther declares it to be 'the seed of Müntzer's and Carlstadt's spirit' to think 'that the divine Word must set forth nothing but spiritual things and have nothing to do with outward, material things'. For such a spirit, civil government, being outward, is of no avail. It was so for Müntzer, and 'this fanatical spirit must remain seditious and murderous'.[21] The transition from the sacramentarian disregard for the externals of the eucharist (he is writing against Oecolampadius and Zwingli) to the rejection of the external civil order was a natural one for Luther. He had seen it in Müntzer, and he feared it in all *Schwärmer*.

In Carlstadt and the Zwickau Prophets it had taken the form of nurturing popular aspirations for radical reform. The Prophets were laymen, gained a following in house meetings in Zwickau and deliberately identified with the simple folk, for example in dress. Carlstadt shed his doctor's degree, donned the grey coat and felt hat of a peasant and wanted to be known only as 'brother Andrew'. His public sermons had fostered popular pressure for drastic measures, and he had allowed the 'disorderly populace' to usurp the role of the authorities by removing images from Wittenberg churches. Was the mob also to take to itself the implementation of other Old Testament laws, such as the execution of adulterers? It was always dangerous to bring the 'disorderly masses' into such an issue. 'Due to great fulness of the spirit they forget civil discipline and manners' and will soon give vent to rioting. Luther had a fundamental mistrust of people at large in matters of reli-

---

21. *That These Words of Christ,* LW 37: 135, 137; WA 23: 261-263.

gion. He despised praise lavished by Anabaptists on the simple and unlearned. They were a seditious mob, lacking the learned men to write books against him.[22]

Oyer points out that, whereas for Justus Menius, the leading Lutheran polemicist against the Anabaptists, their cardinal error was works-righteousness, Luther nearly always related the Anabaptist insistence on the ethic of the Sermon on the Mount to the danger of disturbing the social order.[23] Not only did they abandon their families and teach that all property should be held in common and that no Christian should exercise political rule, but by their preaching among the population secretively and without an authorised call they subverted 'the order of offices and callings'. Luther levelled the same charge against the Zwickau Prophets and Carlstadt.

The Importance of the Call to Preach
Against the papal hierarchy Luther stressed the priesthood of all believers, but against the *Schwärmer* he emphasised the importance of regularly called and ordained ministers. An open letter of 1532 encouraging magisterial action against Anabaptist preachers is called *Infiltrating and Clandestine Preachers* (in Oyer's rendering, *Concerning Sneaks and Corner-Preachers*). 'The Holy Spirit does not come with stealth. He descends in full view from heaven. The serpents glide unnoticed. The doves fly. You can be sure that this secretiveness is characteristic of the devil.'[24] Ignoring the fact that persecution drove the Anabaptists underground, Luther regarded their stealthiness as treachery.

More significantly, such *Schwärmer* lacked a call. In a letter to Melanchthon in early 1522 while Luther was still

22. *Against the Heavenly Prophets, LW* 40: 88ff., 101, 102ff., 162, 211; *WA* 18: 71ff., 84, 85ff., 152, 201; *Table Talk* No. 2838b, tr. T. G. Tappert, *LW* 54: 174; *WA Tisch.* 3: 18.
23. *Op.cit.*, pp. 126-131.
24. Tr. C. Bergendoff, *LW* 40: 384; *WA* 30: III: 518. Cf. Oyer *op.cit.*, pp. 128-129.

at the Wartburg, the latter set down how the spirits of Zwickau were to be tested. They were certainly not to be accepted on their own word. God never sent anyone, not even his own Son, unless called through men or attested by signs. The Old Testament prophets had their authority from the law and the prophetic order.[25] Luther allows for exceptions from the standard procedure, but

> if such mischief is to occur 'out of the inner call of God', then it is necessary that it be proved with miraculous signs. For God does not change his old order for a new one unless the change is accompanied with great signs. Therefore one can believe no one who relies on his own spirit and inner feelings for authority and who outwardly storms against God's accustomed order, unless he therewith performs miraculous signs.

Carlstadt could show no such signs.[26] His calling in Wittenberg was to preach in the Castle Church, not in Luther's pulpit in the Parish Church, and he had no teaching authority outside the University of Wittenberg. He nevertheless refused the summons to return there from Orlamünde.[27]

When the *Schwärmer* appealed to 1 Corinthians 14, Luther countered with his own exegesis. In verses 26ff., Paul is speaking of prophets who are 'teachers who have the office of preaching in the Churches'. Luther is horrified at the suggestion that anyone in the congregation had the right to interrupt the preacher! Did not verse 16 refer explicitly to the 'laity' responding with 'Amen'? Luther believed that the prophets actually sat among the people, and that one prophet might add to what another had said, as in Acts 15:12ff.[28]

25. Tr. G. Krodel, *LW* 48: 366; *WA Briefe* 2: 424-425.
26. *Against the Heavenly Prophets, LW* 40: 113, 222; *WA* 18: 96-97, 213.
27. Cf. Edwards, *art.cit.*, pp. 129, 131; *Against the Heavenly Prophets*, *LW* 40: 111; *WA* 18: 94.
28. *Infiltrating and Clandestine Preachers*, *LW* 40: 388-392; *WA* 30:III: 522-525.

Whereas Carlstadt had demitted his doctorate and refused henceforth to take part in graduations at Wittenberg, Luther declared:

> I would not exchange my doctor's degree for all the world's gold. For I would surely in the long run lose courage and fall into despair if, as these infiltrators, I had undertaken these great and serious matters without call or commission.[29]

It has been argued that Luther's 'doctor-consciousness' (*Doktoratsbewusstsein*) came into renewed prominence in the face of the 'growing menace of religious radicalism'.[30]

Revelations and Distresses

This insistence on a legitimate call meant that Luther would not countenance the appeal of the *Schwärmer* to special elevating experiences of the Spirit. The 1522 letter to Melanchthon has much to say on this subject.[31]

> In order to explore [the prophets'] individual spirit, you should enquire whether they have experienced spiritual distress and the divine birth, death and hell. If you should hear that all [their experiences] are pleasant, quiet, devout (as they say) and spiritual, then don't approve of them, even if they should say that they were caught up to the third heaven. The sign of the Son of Man is then missing, which is the only touchstone of Christians, and a certain differentiator between the spirits.

True conversations with God, like the Old Testament prophets' and Psalmists', are charged with grief, dismay and rejection. The dreams and visions of the saints horrify those who experience them.

29. *Ibid.*, *LW* 40: 387-388; *WA* 30:III:522.
30. B.A. Gerrish, '*Doctor*. Doctor Martin Luther. Subjectivity and Doctrine in the Lutheran Reformation', in Brooks (ed.), *op. cit.*, pp. 8-10. Gerrish reports the conclusions of Steinlein, but if the re-emergence of Luther's 'doctor-consciousness' belongs to the end of the 1520s, this seems rather late as a response to increasing *Schwärmerei*.
31. *LW* 48: 366-367; *WA Br.*2: 425.

As if the [Divine] Majesty could speak familiarly with the Old Adam without first killing him and drying him out so that his horrible stench would not be so foul, since God is a consuming fire.

Even angels frightened Daniel and Mary. God speaks to us indirectly, through men, the way he spoke to Samuel through Eli. Our 'nature cannot bear even a small glimmer of God's [direct] speaking'. When Luther counsels Melanchthon 'Do not even listen to [prophets] if they speak of the glorified Jesus, unless you have first seen the crucified [in them]', we are aware that the issue touches the heart of his theological being. As he said once at table,

> I didn't learn my theology all at once. I had to ponder over it ever more deeply, and my spiritual trials were of help to me in this, for one does not learn anything without practice. This is what the *Schwärmer* and sects lack. They don't have the right adversary, the devil. He would teach them well.[32]

Luther often comments derisively on the spiritual pretensions of the *Schwärmer*. 'They juggle with their "living voice from heaven", their "laying off the material", "sprinkling", "mortification", and similar high-sounding words.'[33] 'They come from heaven, and hear God himself speaking to them as to angels. What is taught at Wittenberg concerning faith and love and the cross of Christ is an unimportant thing. "You yourself must hear the voice of God", they say, "and experience the work of God in you and feel how much your talents weigh".'[34] Carlstadt, who 'devoured the Holy Spirit, feathers and all', and boasts of speaking daily with God in pure fellowship,'is sufficiently wise and articulate, and able to anticipate the future so as to indicate in words everything which

32 *Table Talk* No. 352, *LW* 54: 50; *WA Tisch.* 1: 147.
33. *Letter to the Christians at Strasbourg. In Opposition to the Fanatic Spirit* (1524), tr. Bergendoff, *LW* 40: 70; *WA* 15: 396.
34. *Letter to the Princes of Saxony Concerning the Rebellious Spirit* (1524), tr. Bergendoff, *LW* 40: 50; *WA* 15: 211.

is commanded or forbidden'.[35] But Luther has sharper weapons in his armoury than irony and sarcasm. Characteristic theological judgments are passed on the claims the *Schwärmer* made for their inward spiritual experiences.

Relapse into Works-Righteousness

Luther attacked Carlstadt on many counts. He was silent about 'the main points of Christian doctrine' - how we are to become free from our sins, obtain a good conscience, and win a peaceful heart before God. Instead, he inculcated a new legalism, by forcing laws on the conscience and destroying Christian freedom, both requiring what God does not require and forbidding what God does not forbid, 'making sin where there neither can nor should be any sin'.[36] Furthermore, he used 'unusual new words to excite, terrify and mislead consciences'. That is to say, he propounded, in terms that bewildered Luther, a special kind of mystical experience which Luther judged to be a strenuous human effort at self-mortification.

> They pay no attention to God's design of inward things, such as faith. They ... force all external words and Scriptures belonging to the inward life and faith into new forms of putting to death the old Adam. They invent such things as 'turning from the material', 'concentration', 'adoration', 'self-abstraction', and other such foolishness which has not an inkling of foundation in Scripture. . . What Christ has . . . referred to the inner life of faith, this man applies to outward self-contrived works, even to the point of making the Lord's Supper and the recognition and remembrance of Christ a human work, whereby we in like manner, in 'passionate ardour' and (as they stupidly put it) with 'outstretched desire', put ourselves to death.

---

35. *Against the Heavenly Prophets*, *LW* 40: 83, 116, 133, 132; *WA* 18: 66, 99, 115, 114.
36. *Ibid.*, *LW* 40: 222-223, 82-83, 91, 128-130; *WA* 18: 213-214, 64-66, 73, 111-112.

This spirit always reverses the order of God. 'That which God has made a matter of inward faith and spirit they convert into a human work. But what God has ordained as an outward word and sign and work they convert into an inner spirit.'[37] This second charge we will come to shortly. The first goes very deep indeed, into the abyss itself.

Carlstadt refrains from using the word 'faith' in order to appear 'as if he were teaching other and much higher things than we, and as if true faith was nothing compared to "ardent knowledge"'. He makes much of a 'passionate, heartfelt, earnest knowledge of the body of Christ' in the sacrament.

> But suppose your knowledge and remembrance of Christ were this pure passion, pure heart, pure ardour, pure fire, before which also the sectarian spirits were to melt away and were to blow up their spirituality with words which are a thousand times more high-sounding, what then? What would be gained? Nothing except new monks and hypocrites who would with greater devotion and earnestness stand before the bread and wine . . . as hitherto the sensitive consciences have stood before the sacrament. Indeed as great a concern and anxiety would manifest itself about this knowledge and remembrance,

as Luther the monk had once known.[38] He alleges that Carlstadt's peculiar elaboration of an experiential apprehension of Christ's passion overthrew *sola fide* and established a novel ground for human self-confidence before God that was every bit as doom-laden as the old Catholic religiosity.

The Anabaptists also failed the same critical test in Luther's eyes. There was active among them a *Werkteufel*, literally, a 'work devil', that is, a devil who promoted confidence in works. As under the papacy with the mass, so now with believers' baptism; reception was the key thing, a finished and complete *work*. This shift from the righteousness of faith to the righteousness of works showed

37. *Ibid.*, *LW* 40: 148-149; *WA* 18: 139.
38. *Ibid.*, *LW* 40: 204-208; *WA* 18: 194-198.

that 'We Germans are and remain true Galatians'.[39] Luther also detected in believers' baptism a reliance on faith, chiefly of the one being baptised but also of the baptiser. Among the *Table Talk* we find the comment that, like the Waldensians, the Anabaptists make the sacraments rest on the faith of the persons involved. It is crucial to 'distinguish between the work of God and the work of man'.[40] In his letter *Concerning Rebaptism* he argues that 'There is quite a difference between having faith on the one hand, and depending on one's faith and making baptism depend on faith on the other'.[41]

The Insecurity of Faith
If you make baptism dependent on the faith of the one being baptised or of the baptiser you will never baptise anyone or receive baptism from anyone. How can we be sure that, at the precise moment of baptising, even the apostle Peter had faith? What if the one rebaptised as a believer decides tomorrow or later that at the time of rebaptism he did not really believe? Will he be baptised a third time, because 'now for the first time I feel I have the right faith'? Always something is lacking in faith. The devil can multiply unsettling scruples, says Luther, because he did it with me over confession. 'I never seemed able to confess sufficiently well, 'because we sought to rely on our confession, as those to be baptized now want to rely on their faith'.[42]

Luther has a direct theological interest in this aspect of the controversy with Anabaptism. Of course baptism could not depend on faith if it remained valid even when wrongly given or received without faith. If the Anabaptists proved that children did not have faith, this would not invalidate infant baptisms.[43] Of more relevance to our enquiry is that

39. *Concerning Rebaptism, LW* 40: 248-249; *WA* 26: 161-162.
40. No. 650, *LW* 54: 113-114; *WA Tisch.* 1: 306.
41. *LW* 40: 252; *WA* 26:164.
42. *Concerning Rebaptism, LW* 40: 239-240, 247-248, 250; *WA* 26: 154-155, 161, 163.
43. *Ibid., LW* 40: 246-248; *WA* 26: 160-161.

fundamental conviction of Luther's that surfaces here, that religious experience is always ambiguous. We must believe, but 'we neither should nor can know it for certain'. Often he who claims to believe, does not believe, and he who is in despair, believes. The truth is the opposite of Anabaptism. 'The most certain form of baptism is child baptism . . . For an adult might deceive . . . But a child cannot deceive.'[44]

Luther contrasted the uncertainty of faith with the certainty of baptism. 'Baptism is a God-given thing, instituted and commanded by God himself.' True faith declares, 'On the strength of this command I dare to be baptised'. Since in baptism the Word of God is greater than faith, if faith is lacking one should urge a 'rebelieving' not a rebaptising - Anabelievers, not Anabaptists.[45] It is because baptism rests on God's Word that it is to be accepted as real even if wrongly given or received - and not repeated.[46]

It is Luther's most persistent complaint against *Schwärmer* of all kind, that they paid inadequate regard to the objective work and Word of God. They were always bothered about the involvement of unworthy persons in the sacraments, and would not let them 'be grounded and administered simply in God's words and commands'.[47] 'Christ is ever beneficial, wherever he is, however he may seem of no avail because of my unbelief. The sun is always shining, though unseen by the blind man . . . the body of Christ is always in the sacrament.'[48]

Inwardness and Reason Above the Bible
'It is the nature of this spirit', wrote Luther against Carlstadt, 'to pay no attention to the external Word and sign of God'. Carlstadt's cavalier treatment of the Words of

44. *Ibid.*, *LW* 40: 241, 244; *WA* 26: 155, 157.
45. *Ibid.*, *LW* 40: 255, 259, 253, 260-261; *WA* 26: 167, 171, 165, 172-173.
46. *Confession*, *LW* 37: 366; *WA* 26: 506.
47. *Ibid.*, *LW* 37: 188; *WA* 26: 288.
48. *Against the Heavenly Prophets*, *LW* 40: 205; *WA* 18: 194-195.

Institution was of a piece with his general preference for his own wisdom rather than the words of Scripture. 'If Scripture will not help, my big head will, for it is full of spirit.'[49] Yet however implausible Carlstadt's biblical interpretation might appear, he scarcely deserved to be classed with Schwenckfeld and Müntzer in their explicit devaluation of Scripture.

> This devil [Schwenckfeld] stalks about boldly and without disguise and teaches us openly to disregard Scripture, just as Müntzer and Carlstadt also did, who developed their wisdom out of the witness of their 'inwardness', and needed the Holy Scriptures not for themselves but only for the instruction of others, as an external witness in their 'inwardness'.[50]

But Luther is not interested in drawing distinctions among the children of the devil. Oecolampadius and Zwingli abuse Scripture just like Müntzer. Carlstadt and Zwingli had their beliefs fixed before ever they searched the Scriptures for support, which they got by forcing them to fit their own notions. 'It is not the fanatics' practice to rely upon the Scriptures', Luther claims against the sacramentarians of Zürich and Basel.

> My wretched fanatics are still too inexperienced to be able to despise good insights and thoughts. Therefore they think, when they dream something up, it is forthwith the Holy Spirit. Oh, how many fine insights I have had into the Scriptures which I have had to let go, whereas, if a fanatic had had them, all the printers in the world would have been too few for him.[51]

Had not Zwingli recently acquired fresh biblical support for his position through a dream? Repeatedly Luther accuses

---

49. *Ibid.*, *LW* 40: 177, 179; *WA* 18: 166, 169.
50. *Confession, LW* 37: 290; *WA* 26: 434.
51. *That These Words of Christ, LW*, 37: 139,47,52,45; *WA* 23: 265,117,125,113. Luther later contradicts himself when he argues, *ad hominem*, that the fanatics did not get their beliefs from the Spirit before they physically and outwardly heard or read them (*LW* 37: 137; *WA* 23:263).

his opponents of distorting the plain sense of Scripture by letting human reason determine what it could or could not mean. So although on one level Luther conducted the Supper-strife as a debate about correct exegesis, he could not accept that the *Schwärmer* were capable of understanding Scripture aright. Their misconceptions predisposed them to handle the words of God corruptly. They assigned too high a value to their inner experience, depreciated the external Word and in general failed to recognise the essential dependence of the inward and spiritual upon the outward and material. This last failing was common to all the *Schwärmer*. It evoked from Luther many of the passages of most lasting significance in his polemical writings against them.

The Inward Given Only Through the Outward

From what Luther repeatedly asserted against *Schwärmer* of all varieties, it is difficult to believe that he could have accepted the authenticity of any receiving of the Spirit or charismata that was not effected through an outward observance of the Church.

> God deals with us in a twofold manner, first outwardly, then inwardly. Outwardly he deals with us through the oral word of the gospel and through material signs, that is, baptism and the sacrament of the altar. Inwardly he deals with us through the Holy Spirit, faith and other gifts. But whatever their measure or order the outward factors should and must precede. The inward experience follows and is effected by the outward. God has determined to give the inward to no one except through the outward.[52]

Thus Luther wrote in 1525 against Carlstadt, who reversed God's order and claimed to proceed not through the external Word to the spirit but from the spirit to the exter-

---

52. *Against the Heavenly Prophets*, LW 40: 146; WA 18: 136. Cf. *Confession* (LW 37: 368; WA 26: 507): the forgiveness of sins is received in the Church through the preaching of the gospel, baptism and the sacrament of the altar.

nal Word. Carlstadt cites the promise of the Paraclete in John 15: 26-27 - as if the apostles received the Spirit without Christ's external Word! 'Such an exalted spirit which is above the apostles ought also forsooth demonstrate his superiority by great signs', but he is as incapable of proving his spirit and inward witness with signs as of proving his teaching with Scripture.[53] Luther does not deny that God *could* have chosen to bestow spiritual life apart from material things, but his will is in fact to give it through the humanity of Christ, through the Word, which in this context is an outward reality, and through the material sacramental signs. The Spirit cannot be with us except in material and physical things such as the Word, water and Christ's body and in his saints on earth. So far from the truth is the belief that 'nothing spiritual can be present where there is anything material and physical'.[54]

This emphasis was, of course, of central importance in Luther's refutation of the sacramentarians in the Supperstrife. The details of its application need not concern us here, but we must note his conviction that, in exposing the fallacies of Oecolampadius and others, he was involved in the same task as faced him with Müntzer and Carlstadt. This is evident from his references back to his writings against the latter pair, especially *Against the Heavenly Prophets*. Not that Luther obscured all the differences among the *Schwärmer*. Schwenckfeld 'vehemently blasphemed the external Word as unsuitable for belief'. To him 'the Word' was not a spoken utterance but the eternal truth of God.[55] Luther's *Table Talk* mentions 'Anabaptist scoffers at the oral Word' and sacramentarians who claim that nothing external is salvatory (which might be true of man's externals but not of God's).[56] The sacramentarians alleged that 'the divine Word must set forth nothing but

53. *Against the Heavenly Prophets, LW* 40: 195; *WA* 18: 185.
54. *That These Words of Christ, LW* 37: 140, 95; *WA* 23: 267-269, 193.
55. *Confession, LW* 37: 293; *WA* 26: 436.
56. No. 4081 (*LW* 54: 318; *WA Tisch.* 4: 121-122).

spiritual things and having nothing to do with outward, material things'. The reverse was the case.

> God sets before us no word or commandment without including with it something material and outward, and proffering it to us ... You will find no word of God in the entire Scriptures in which something material and outward is not contained and presented.

To Abraham God gave with his Word Isaac, to Noah the rainbow. So 'the outward things connected with God's Word are salvation and blessedness, because they inhere in the Word and bind our faith ... Abraham had to attach his faith to the coming Isaac' because Isaac was 'connected with the Word'.[57]

In the Lord's Supper, God 'joined both together, the Word and his body, to be eaten spiritually with the heart and physically with the mouth'. God is present *for us* 'when he adds his Word and binds himself, saying, "Here you are to find me" ... When you eat this you eat my body, and nowhere else. Why? Because I wish to attach myself here with my Word, in order that you may not have to buzz about, trying to seek me in all the places where I am.'[58] It is the goal of the devil to do away with the entire sacrament and all the outward ordinances of God. Then 'all that would count would be for the heart to stare inwardly at the spirit'. 'Should you ask how one gains access to this same lofty spirit they do not refer you to the outward gospel but to some imaginary realm, saying, "Remain in 'self-abstraction' where I now am and you will have the same experience. A heavenly voice will come, and God himself will speak to you".' Carlstadt 'tears down the bridge, the path, the way, the ladder, and all the means by which the Spirit might come to you', and instead would have you come to

---

57. *That These Words of Christ,* LW 37: 135-136; WA 23: 261-163. Luther refers back to this passage in his *Confession Concerning Christ's Supper,* LW 37: 292; WA 26: 436.
58. *That These Words of Christ,* LW 37: 88, 68-69; WA 23: 181-183, 151-153.

the Spirit and 'learn how to journey on the clouds and ride on the wind'. The remembrance commanded by Christ is for Carlstadt entirely a matter of 'inner thoughts of the heart'. For Luther it is oral proclamation (1 Cor. 11:26), public commemoration, as in the Psalms of Israel's worship. If one owned a treasure chest that was buried, 'I might think myself to death and experience all desire, great passion and ardour in such knowledge and remembrance of the treasure until I became ill', but all to no avail. The chest has to be opened and the treasure handled.[59]

False Notions of 'Spirit' and 'Flesh'
Having demolished God's external order, Carlstadt has erected his own with his new legalism in worship and behaviour. With his remarkable facility for suggestive connections between old error and new, Luther pinpoints the root of both in a misunderstanding of the nature of the spiritual and the fleshly. Luther's critique reflects his recovery of a Hebraic understanding of 'spirit', whereas the *Schwärmer*'s outlook betrayed the influence of the Greek tradition, in which almost by definition spirit was other than material. While Carlstadt makes everything spiritual that God has made bodily, the pope transforms spiritual Christianity into an outward bodily community. 'We proceed between the two, making nothing spiritual or bodily, but keeping spiritual what God makes spiritual, and bodily what he makes bodily.'[60] The fatal mistake of the *Schwärmer* was to suppose that spiritual eating or drinking was eating or drinking a spiritual object rather than in a spiritual way. Twice in one of his major diatribes against the likes of Zwingli Luther quotes a Latin tag, 'Spirit consists in the use, not in the object'. 'All that our body does outwardly and physically, if God's Word is added to it and it is done through faith, is in reality and in name done spir-

---

59. *Against the Heavenly Prophets, LW* 40: 191, 207-208, 213; *WA* 18: 181, 197, 203.
60. *Ibid., LW* 40: 147-148, 192; *WA* 18: 137-138, 181.

itually ... The "spiritual" is nothing else than what is done in us and by us through the Spirit and faith, whether the object with which we are dealing is physical or spiritual.' Mary spiritually conceived and bore the physical Christ. 'Christ's body and flesh are quite compatible with the Spirit.' Whenever in the Bible spirit and 'flesh' are opposed, it is the old, sinful flesh that is meant, not the human body. Indeed, so far from Christ's flesh being of no avail (according to the *Schwärmer's* frequent appeal to John 6:63), when it is eaten 'physically and spiritually, the food is so powerful that it transforms us into itself, and out of fleshly, sinful, mortal men makes spiritual, holy, living men'.[61] This was the complete antithesis of Zwingli's view that the soul was saved only by Christ's divine nature. In an interesting eucharistic *communicatio idiomatum*, Luther declares that both mouth and heart eat Christ's body, the mouth physically for the heart, and the heart spiritually for the mouth.[62]

So 'to worship in the spirit is to worship spiritually, in a spiritual manner, whether Christ is in heaven, on earth, in the sacrament, or anywhere else'.[63] The course of controversy has markedly changed Luther's emphasis. Whereas, in the years of his assault upon the Babylonian captivity of the mass, and even as late as the series of eight *'Invocavit' Sermons* he preached against the Wittenberg radicals in March 1522, immediately on his return from the Wartburg, he stressed the great difference between outward and inward reception (a mouse can receive Christ's body outwardly), and could say that 'Christianity consists solely in faith, and no outward work must be attached to it',[64] now he insists that nowhere but in the Church's Word and sacraments will Christ or the Spirit be received.

---

61. *That These Words of Christ*, LW 37: 89-101; WA 23: 183-205.
62. *Ibid.*, LW 37: 93; WA 23: 191.
63. *Confession*, LW 37: 284; WA 26: 427.
64. *Sixth Sermon*, tr. J. W. Doberstein, *LW* 51: 92; WA 10:III: 49.

Lutheran Critique of Charismatics

Luther's developed emphasis on the inseparability of Spirit from the Word and sacrament of the Church has been taken up by present-day Lutherans in evaluating the distinctive features of the charismatic movement. 'The emphasis of our Lutheran heritage on the external Word as the instrument of the Holy Spirit helps prevent a subjectivism that seeks divine comfort and strength through an interior experience rather than in the objective word of the Gospel.'[65] 'An individual's experience of the Holy Spirit is not immediate ... God works through means: the Word and sacraments. To deny that is eventually to fly in the face of the incarnate Word, for the Holy Spirit is the Spirit of the incarnate Son.'[66] *Solo verbo* (by the Word alone) is as basic to biblical and Lutheran doctrine as *sola gratia*.[67] The seeking of assurance based on signs such as tongues rather than on the objective promises of the gospel imports an element of subjectivity alien to Lutheran faith.[68] Christian certainty is to be grounded on God's faithfulness to his promise, not on feelings or faith, for 'In the Lutheran understanding of experience, so vividly portrayed in Luther himself, all experience, including the experience of faith itself, is ambiguous . . . [This] ambiguity is experienced as the simultaneous presence of original sin and the promise of grace ... How is this essential ambiguity in the Christian life expressed in the charismatic movement's description of charismatic experiences?'[69] (To such a question it might be said in reply that Luther's emphasis too easily becomes a self centred circularity – 'I am a sinner ... but forgiven, ... a sinner ... forgiven', – inhibiting the freedom to serve others. Charismatic teaching

---

65. McDonnell, vol. 1, p. 352, Lutheran Church Missouri Synod, 1972.
66. *Ibid.*, vol. 1, p. 564, Lutheran Church in America, 1974.
67. *Ibid.*, vol. 1, p. 309, Missouri Synod, 1977.
68. *Ibid.*, vol. 2, p. 17, Missouri Synod, 1975.
69. *Ibid.*, vol. 2, pp. 445-446, Lutheran Council in the U.S.A., 1978.

stresses just such a *release*, grounded on a renewed awareness of Christian assurance.)

Other points are made with less emphasis. The Spirit is received solely by grace, not because of any effort or deed on the part of the recipient. According to the Lutheran Confessions the fullness of the Spirit is bestowed in conversion and baptism. They do not countenance a basis for Church fellowship in a common experience of 'baptism with the Spirit'. The Lutheran tradition has usually interpreted the charismata as experiences occurring only in the apostolic Church.

At the same time some of these Lutheran assessments acknowledge possible weaknesses in Lutheranism that may have been ripe for correction by charismatics. Have not Lutherans been over-dominated by 'a Second-Article mentality', a preoccupation with Christ to the neglect of the Spirit, or, to put it in another way, by an emphasis on justification that ignores sanctification? Conjoined with the latter has been an undue focussing on the sacramental rite itself with failure to appreciate baptism's paradigmatic function as the pattern for the whole life of the Christian. Such a criticism does not imply that the charismatic remedy is necessarily the right one; a better response may be rather the recovery of Luther's teaching on the baptismal character of the whole Christian life.[70] The concern with sacramental objectivity may have fostered a mistrust of emotional or experiential manifestations of life in the Spirit. Linked with this may be the comment that 'Luther's high estimation of confession (*Beichte*) was never accepted theologically, nor reflected in the praxis of the Church'.[71]

Moreover, the renewal movement itself may not be without precedent in the Lutheran Churches. Charismatic

70. *Ibid.*, vol. 1, p. 371 (American Lutheran Church, 1973), 554 (Lutheran Church in America, 1974), with McDonnell's comment, p. 548.
71. *Ibid.*, vol. 1, p. 554; vol. 2, p. 459, Lutheran Churches in German Democratic Republic, 1978.

LUTHER'S QUARREL WITH THE *SCHWÄRMER*

Christianity stands in a tradition stretching back via Pentecostalism, the Holiness movement and Methodism to the Moravians and Pietists in German Lutheranism in the seventeenth and eighteenth centuries. Pietism stressed among other things the centrality of personal devotion and a knowledge of God anchored in the heart rather than the head. It sought a revival of practical and missionary lay Christianity in an age of arid confessional orthodoxy.

In turn a question is raised which none of these Lutheran assessments faces, whether Luther himself did not put 'a questionable stamp of religious subjectivity on the Lutheran version of Christian faith'.[72] B. A. Gerrish believes that 'this can readily be verified by noting how his experience of God is canonized in the Lutheran confessions'.[73] James Atkinson's recent passionate plea for the Catholic Church to receive Luther back into the fold argues that it is Luther's personal experience of *sola gratia*, rather than any particular articulation of the doctrine of justification, that affords the greatest hope of reconciliation.[74] Although Gerrish defends Luther against the charges of subjectivity made by Catholic scholars such as Lortz, he accepts that the Reformer's strict correlation of subject and object, whereby God and faith belong together because Word and faith are correlatives, accompanied a new interest in the religious subject. 'The content of doctrine is precisely religious subjectivity', for as Luther put it, 'The proper subject of theology is man guilty of sin and condemned, and God the justifier and saviour of man the sinner'.[75] Perhaps in the end Luther is fitted to be the

---

72. *Ibid.*, vol 1, p. 551, Lutheran Church in America, 1974.
73. *Art. cit.*, p. 13.
74. *Martin Luther: Prophet to the Church Catholic*, Exeter, 1983.
75. *Art. cit.*, pp. 12-13, 18-19; Luther, *Commentary on Psalm 51*, tr. J. Pelikan, *LW* 12: 311; *WA* 40:II: 328.

charismatic movement's 'cure' partly because he is also its long-distant 'cause'.⁷⁶

76. One can of course collect from Luther's writings and career indications that not all things charismatic would have been anathema to him. It is arguable that the priesthood of all believers needs to be undergirded by the gifts of the Spirit if it is to function aright. In the *Preface* to *The German Mass and Order of Service* of 1526 Luther expressed his yearning for informal gatherings of those 'who wanted to be Christians in earnest' in terms not dissimilar to many contemporary renewal groups (*LW* 53: 63-64; *WA* 19: 75). In his writings of 1523 on the ministry and the congregation he assigned a responsibility to all Christians, as priests by baptism, to judge the teaching of ordained clergy, and declared that if a Church member brings forth something from Scripture that confounds the teaching of the official minister, then God's authority is found with that member (cf. *That a Christian Assembly or Congregation Has the Right and Power to Judge all Teaching . . .* , *WA* 11: 408-416; *LW* 39: 301-314; *Concerning the Ministry*, *WA* 12: 169-195; *LW* 40: 3-44; *Letter to the Christians of Leisnig*, *WA* 12:11-30). The role that he accorded to the *paterfamilias* in the Christian education of his household shows that the laity were by no means wholly disenfranchised, even in his later writings, from the teaching of the Word. He could even on occasion give heed to the guidance afforded by his wife's dreams, but out of personal regard, not because he respected dreams in general as channels of divine admonition. Indeed, all indications of the kind noted here remain either isolated and rather exceptional or early and largely corrected or eclipsed in Luther's later output. They cannot be allowed to offset the consistent thrust of his anti-*Schwärmer* writings. B.R. Hoffman argues forcefully in *Luther and the Mystics* (Minneapolis, 1976) that interpreters of Luther have consistently underestimated the place of mystical experience in his life. Hoffman's study is misleadingly titled. He uses 'mystical' in a broad sense, of inner heart-experience of the presence of Christ. The repeated 'Damnant Anabaptistas' of the *Augsburg Confession* survives as an embarrassment to many a subscribing Lutheran today, not solely among those influenced by charismatic renewal. The treatment of the Anabaptists by the magisterial Reformers remains to be formally repented of by the Churches of the Reformation in an ecumenical era.

CHRISTIAN EXPERIENCE AND DIVINE REVELATION IN THE THEOLOGIES OF FRIEDRICH SCHLEIERMACHER AND KARL BARTH

ALAN TORRANCE

Friedrich Schleiermacher and Karl Barth hold in common the honour of being widely considered the two greatest reformed theologians since John Calvin.[1] Yet they could hardly be more different in their theological method, presuppositions and conclusions. This disparity is often misconstrued due to popular and often inaccurate cameo-impressions of their theology. The former is considered the champion of Christian experience while the latter is conceived to be the exemplary and coldly systematic theologian of revelation. However, two things should become clear from close examination of the writings of both these men. On the one hand, the conception of piety and religious feeling lying at the heart of Schleiermacher's theology is very different indeed from the common understanding of Christian experience. On the other hand, Barth's understanding of revelation commits him to giving human experience a place of central importance in his theology – and yet his overriding concern is to operate with a profoundly *holistic* conception of human experience as it is addressed by God, and to avoid the common mistake of emphasising one form of experience at the cost of others.

In seeking to understand the radical differences between the two great men, the reader must bear in mind the profoundly different contexts and specific concerns of their theological approaches. Schleiermacher was writing as the

1. Even critics like von Frank and Werner Elert find it difficult to avoid Lülmann's description of Schleiermacher in *Schleiermacher der Kirchenvater des 19. Jahrhunderts* as 'the genius of the 19th century in the religious, ecclesiastical and theological field'. K. Barth, *The Theology of Schleiermacher*, Eng. trans. Edinburgh, 1982, pp. xiv-xv.

Christian apologist seeking to offer more than simply a defence of the faith, but rather, positive apologetics – the advocacy of the Christian faith construed in terms congenial to the intellectual living in a period characterised by the decaying Enlightenment, the flood-tide of Romanticism and Kantian-Fichtian idealism – a time of surging crosscurrents of thought and the radical questioning of traditional approaches to all spheres of life. Barth on the other hand was writing as the theologian-churchman who had witnessed (and continued to witness in the rise of the Third Reich) the detrimental compromise of theology by the demands of German culture and the vacillating fashions of nineteenth-century philosophy. His concern was to allow the methods and categories operative in his theology to be moulded radically and rigorously by the Word of God, by God's unique and full self-revelation in Christ as the eternal Word made flesh – what is variously described as Barth's Christocentrism or Christomonism, depending on the particular sympathies of the commentator!

To contrast the contexts in which these two men are writing is not in any way to seek to detract from or conceal the radical opposition of their respective approaches to which Barth gives unambiguous expression when he writes, 'I have indeed no reason to conceal the fact that I view with mistrust both Schleiermacher and all that Protestant theology became under his influence, that in Christian matters I do *not* regard the decision that was made in that intellectually and culturally significant age as a happy one and that the result of my study of Schleiermacher thus far may be summed up in that saying of Goethe: Lo, his spirit calls to thee from a cave: be a man and do *not* follow me.'[2] That having been said, however, we could not do better in interpreting them than to seek to follow Barth's hermeneutical way of love since, as he writes in the introduction to his Schleiermacher lectures, 'love, when one can love, is a relatively surer way to

2. *Ibid.*, pp. xv-xvi.

knowledge than alienation or aversion'.[3] Barth is profoundly true to this in his interpretation of Schleiermacher and seeks, despite his deep-rooted opposition to his theological method, to be as open and positive as he can, insisting that 'the aim of my lectures is not to make you hard on the universally venerated Schleiermacher but to see and know and learn to understand him with you, not to induce the arrogant view that you can become a match for him but to handle him modestly, not to condemn him but to comprehend him as he was and had to be.'[4] Herein lies the ground of his forthright criticism of Brunner's almost unrestrained attack on Schleiermacher and also his reputation as one of the finest and most accurate interpreters of Schleiermacher. Oh that Barth's attitude to the interpretation of other theologians were adopted by those who have written on Barth's own theology! Too often both 'evangelicals' and 'liberals' alike have failed to have that scientific objectivity which Barth believed to be so important.

SCHLEIERMACHER

Despite the dangers of a genetic approach to any theologian (the danger of reading into him the influences you want to find in him and to criticise) in expounding the thought of Schleiermacher I shall attempt to draw a parallel between Schleiermacher and Kant which clarifies Schleiermacher's approach to experience. Immanuel Kant was awakened from what he called his 'dogmatic slumbers' in the barren dogmatic metaphysics of 'dry-as-dust' philosophers like Wolff by David Hume's empiricism and radical criticism of speculative ideas whose origin could not be found in the realm of the experience of the senses. Hume's empirical principles functioned as a 'razor' to cut away metaphysical ideas and principles whose origin could

3. *Ibid.*, p. xvii.
4. *Ibid.*, p. xvi.

not be grounded in experience. Hume therefore put all sorts of terms and ideas in the common parlance and thinking of the time to his acid test – what type of sense experience is responsible for such a term or notion? Can one trace the concept in question to a concrete, verifiable experience or is it just a creation of the imagination without any genuine reference?[5] Suddenly the validity and value of a variety of terms like 'God', 'morals', 'causality' 'spirit', the 'soul', 'self' and so on, had to be subjected to rigorous questioning and analysis as to their source and ultimate meaningfulness and their use was either to be justified by experience or redefined. Kant therefore regarded Hume as a sceptic[6] – not only did his system undermine morality, self-identity and belief in God but also, as Kant saw, the whole of science was threatened by Hume's reduction of the principle of causality simply to the discernment of the constant conjunction between two perceptions and the feeling of necessity in associating these deriving from their constant conjunction. Kant believed the causal principle to be the corner-stone of the entire scientific enterprise. Accordingly, in his *Critique of Pure Reason*, he engaged in what might be termed scien-

5. David Hume wrote anonymously for publication his own *Abstract* of his *Treatise of Human Nature* and I quote from this. 'Whenever any idea is ambiguous he has always recourse to the impression which must render it clear and precise. And when he suspects that any philosophical term has no idea annexed to it (as is too common), he always asks "from what impression that idea is derived?" And if no impression can be produced, he concludes that the term is altogether insignificant. It is after this manner he examines our idea of *substance* and *essence*, and it were to be wished that this rigorous method were more practiced in all philosophical debates.' Antony Flew (ed.), *David Hume on Human Nature and the Understanding*, New York, 1962, p. 291-292.
6. 'It is important to remember .. that Kant saw Hume not as an empiricist, but as a sceptic, one who declared that there was no rational basis for our beliefs about the world, including our scientific beliefs.' W. H. Walsh in *Kant's Criticism of Metaphysics*, Edinburgh, 1975, p. 2.

tific *apologetics* (the attempt to defend science by firmly establishing the causal principle) by seeking to show that the causal principle was inherent in and basic to all coherent experience. One's thought processes *necessarily* determine or interpret experiences on the basis of the law of causality. There could be no coherent experience without this law. It was *a priori* to all coherent experience as it was the principle of synthesis in experience – the principle that held experience together. Kant's genius therefore was to defend certain terms and principles (like cause and causality) by showing that they were essential to the apparatus of experience in the subject and could not therefore be dispensed with despite the fact that these principles themselves were not the objects of an independent sense experience. Contact lenses cannot be seen by the subject when they are in use but they are for many a *sine qua non* of precise, visual experience.

Scheiermacher was profoundly and fundamentally influenced by Kant. Kant's method and his idealism moulded Schleiermacher's approach. Indeed I will suggest that it was precisely the apologetic method which Kant formulated and used on behalf of science, morality and religion over and against what he regarded as Hume's scepticism which Schleiermacher took up and used against Kant himself. Kant had responded to Hume's *Dialogues* and their repudiation of the proofs of the existence of God by designating God a place within the sphere of moral experience. Belief in God was construed as a postulate of, as *a priori* to, the moral life or what he termed 'Practical Reason'. Schleiermacher however rejected the demotion of God to the realm of mere moral experience. For Schleiermacher, who was profoundly influenced by Moravian pietism [7] and its simple but all-embracing love of Jesus (given expression to by men like Zinzendorf and others), religion is in-

---

7. Schleiermacher once said of himself that all his life he had been a 'Moravian of a higher order'. K. Barth, *From Rousseau to Ritschl*, Eng. Trans. London, 1959, p. 332

tegral to the entirety of human experience in all its forms and not simply to one single part of it. At the same time Schleiermacher was influenced by the Moravian pietists' and the Romantics' distaste for dogmatic systems and the elevation of 'pure reason'. They had awakened him out of his dogmatic slumber (leading to the well-known confrontation with what he saw to be the dogmatism of his father) and now he set out to produce an *apologetic*, offering the Christian Faith as something worthwhile in the influential academic and literary circles in which he mixed. What Kant had done for the causal principle and for science he sought to do for Christian piety. And, as in Kant's *Critique of Pure Reason*, this would go hand in hand with the rejection of dogmatism and speculative metaphysical systems which had been initiated by David Hume. For Schleiermacher God was not simply to be found in logical systems of belief or within the sphere of reason or indeed, as Kant had settled for, of moral experience, rather the experience of God was to be seen to be fundamental to and to underpin as its essential ground the very structure of the totality of human experience in all its forms but most specifically in its most supreme form – Christian piety.

Geoffrey Bromiley therefore points to the key to Schleiermacher's approach when he writes that Schleiermacher grounds religion in an 'emotional *a priori*'[8] ('Emotional' I suspect is misleading, 'empirico-existential'[9] would be more accurate if also anachronistic and rather clumsy!). The point is that what Kant had done for science in grounding and defending scientific principles before what he saw to be the philosophical scepticism of his age, Schleiermacher sought to do for religion, in an age which

8. G. W. Bromiley, *Historical Theology: An Introduction*, Edinburgh, 1978, p. 362.
9. A. I. C. Heron emphasis, quite correctly, that Schleiermacher is not building on '"religious experiences of a mystical or emotional kind. ... What he is trying to describe, and to find terms to name, is what would later be called "existential awareness".' *A Century of Protestant Theology*, Guildford, 1980, p. 25.

seemed to be undermining more and more the importance and relevance of religious conviction, by setting out to establish unshakeably the essential principle underlying all piety and religion. This he did by grounding it in the heart of the human life-experience as being *a priori* to and of the essence of the *synthetic unity* of the individual – that which holds the self's experience together as a unity. The inherent compatibility of this approach with the philosophical climate of the time made it particularly attractive. In addition, it had an intrinsic appeal to the contemporary romantic mood in the wider academic and literary scene since it combined a holistic conception of man with the exaltation of the human life-experience and self-consciousness.

Now let us turn to Schleiermacher's own argumentation. Schleiermacher begins *Der Christliche Glaube* with the question: Where is the *home* of Christian piety which forms the basis of all ecclesiastical communions? This is directly parallel to the question David Hume puts to all our ideas to discover whether they are genuine and useful or mere figments of the imagination, the arbitrary creation of idle speculation. It is in answering this question that he will show in Kantian fashion that it stems from the very heart of human experience to the extent that it is truly human. It is part of the essence, ground or grammar of this. But what kind of thing is it?

Is Christian piety a Knowing or a Doing or a Feeling? To answer this he describes life as an alternation between an *abiding-in-self* (*Insichbleiben*) and a *passing-beyond-self* (*Aussichheraustreten*) on the part of the subject.[10] Knowing (as possession of knowledge) and Feeling are part of the subjective abiding-in-self whereas Doing and Knowing-as-act are part of the passing-beyond-oneself.

Piety, he argues, cannot consist in knowing as one cannot measure the amount of piety a person has by the

---

10. Friedrich Schleiermacher, *The Christian Faith*, Eng. trans., Edinburgh, 1928, §3, 3.

amount of knowledge he possesses. Similarly piety cannot consist in Doing since the most contradictory types of action, of Doing, result from piety. The essence of piety is deeper in the self's subjectivity therefore than any form of action or knowledge. It lies so deep within the subject's essence that it is not effected or acted upon by the self: it is part of the self's abiding-in-self and so it must in all its diverse expressions be at root a state of feeling. But it is a special form of feeling, it is not simply a sensual feeling but a feeling relating to self-consciousness. This requires to be explained in terms of a distinction which Schleiermacher makes between two kinds of self-consciousness,[11] namely between:

(1). *the objective consciousness of self* which arises in analytic contemplation as expressed, for example, in self-approval or self-reproach, and

(2). what he sees to be genuine self-consciousness — the self-consciousness that persists unaltered during a series of diverse acts of thinking and willing. This he calls the *subjective self-consciousness*. Schleiermacher is referring here to the self's tacit and continual self-awareness in feeling, thinking and action. This must be present to the extent that in all one's actions one is aware that they originate from and relate directly to oneself. Raising one's arm, for example, can only be described as an action in so far as one is aware that what is being raised is one's *own* arm and that it is *oneself* that is doing the raising. This awareness implies a continual self-consciousness accompanying all one does and it is this which Schleiermacher regards as genuine, self-consciousness. As Schleiermacher himself comments, it is what makes the experience of joy and sorrow *my own* joy and sorrow where the joy or sorrow is experienced in all its immediacy without being analysed or meditated upon.

Accordingly piety has been traced within the subject to the subject's deepest form of human *being* and of the *ways*

---

11. *Ibid.*, §3, 2.

of human being *i.e.* doing, knowing and feeling. It lies behind all knowing or doing: indeed, as a third underlying category of human being, its existence explains why different forms of *doing* can proceed from the same *knowing*. It is so much part of one's inner life that it is unaffected by the subject, part of the subject's abiding-in-self (*Insichbleiben*). It is internal to the structure of one's immediate, spontaneous, totally subjective self-consciousness and as such is not something one can change or alter.

Therefore in Schleiermacher's own words: 'the piety which forms the basis of all ecclesiastical communion is, considered purely in itself, neither a Knowing nor a Doing, but a modification of Feeling or of immediate self-consciousness.'[12] From here he goes on to refine the essence of piety, this modification of feeling, still further: 'The common element in all (however diverse expressions of) piety, ... the self-identical essence of piety, is this: the consciousness of being absolutely dependent, or, which is the same thing, of being in relation with God.'[13]

Schleiermacher attempts to prove this in the following way. We are never simply conscious of a variable state of being, therefore we can identify two elements in consciousness (1) a self-caused element *or* what he also refers to as a Being (*ein Sein*) and (2) a Having-by-some-means-come-to-be (*Ein Irgendwiegewordensein*). This latter causes us to look for an Other, the factor which is the source of this element. Accordingly these two elements express firstly the existence of the subject for itself and secondly its co-existence with an Other.[14] At the same time, he points out a correspondence between these two elements and the subject's receptivity (*Empfänglichkeit*) and activity (*Selbsttätigkeit*) and then goes on to support his deductions by arguing that if we could 'think away the co-existence with an Other, but oth-

12. *Ibid.*, §3, Introductory proposition.
13. *Ibid.*, §4, Introduction proposition
14. *Ibid.*, §4, 1.

erwise think ourselves as we are then a self-consciousness which predominantly expressed an effective condition of receptivity would be impossible and any self-consciousness could then express only activity – an activity which not being directed to any object would be merely an urge outwards, an indefinite agility without form or colour.'[15]

Human receptivity therefore is what makes human action conscious action *i.e.* self-conscious action and is defined in terms of the existence of an Other. Schleiermacher is hereby progressing step by step to a point where he can show that Christian piety is the fullest possible expression of the most fundamental structure of human being or, to put it more simply, what makes a person human. And the propositions from which he argues are discernible to everyone 'capable of a little introspection'![16]

By going deeper into the nature of self-consciousness he finds that basic to the elements of *receptivity* on the one hand and *activity* on the other are to be found the feeling of dependence and the feeling of freedom respectively. Both involve the existence of an Other. This is true of our receptivity because it must be by way of an influence from some other quarter that we have come to such a state. And it is true of our activity because it presupposes an Other in that an Other is determined by our free act. Freedom cannot refer simply to the temporal change and development of a being – the feeling of freedom involves the consciousness that in free activity one stands over and against that which is other. One is never simply free without being free *in relation* to something that is other than the self. It is at this point that a decisive move in Schleiermacher's argument occurs. He argues that this reciprocity between the self and the corresponding Other suggests that if the totality of all our moments of feeling is conceived as a whole, as a unity, then the corresponding

15. *Ibid.*, §4, 1.
16. *Ibid.*, §4, 1.

Other is also to be conceived of as a totality or as one. Now, therefore, a unitary Other has been postulated as *a priori* to the self-consciousness constitutive of selfhood. The Other is postulated because we have no feeling of absolute unlimited freedom, therefore there is always a feeling of dependence, that is of a limitation of our freedom by the Other, that which is Other.

'The self-consciousness which accompanied all our activity and, therefore, since that is never zero, accompanies our whole existence, and negatives absolute freedom, is itself precisely a consciousness that the whole of our spontaneous activity comes from a source outside of us in just the same sense in which anything towards which we have a feeling of absolute dependence would not be possible.'[17]

At this point Schleiermacher quite simply asserts that the *Whence* of our receptive and active existence, as implied in this self-consciousness, is to be designated by the word 'God' – this being the 'really original signification of that word.'[18] This Whence can only be designated 'God' because it cannot be the world or any part of it. Why not? Because (a) we have a feeling of freedom in relation to the world (but not in relation to the Other which is, rather, that which conditions our feeling of freedom); (b) we are parts of the world (and it is not therefore totally Other); (c) we exercise influence on the world, *i.e.* we condition it and; (d) we could conceive of our having an influence upon all its parts.

Therefore Schleiermacher can say that the concept of 'God' is nothing more than the expression of the feeling of absolute dependence. Or to put it in other terms, 'to feel oneself absolutely dependent and to be conscious of being in relation to God is one and the same thing.'[19] God-consciousness and self-consciousness are inseparable. God-

---

17. *Ibid.*, §4, 3.
18. *Ibid.*, §4, 4.
19. *Ibid.*, §4, 4.

consciousness is included in self-consciousness. In so far as this God-consciousness is, as we have already seen, simply a 'consciousness of the Other, it is hard to see, as H. R. Macintosh suggests, how Schleiermacher can escape the charge of pantheism.

What has happened here? Just as Kant by his transcendental method deduced that 'every event has a cause' is a necessary category of all coherent experience, Schleiermacher had deduced by a similar analysis of the structure of conscious experience that God-consciousness is a necessary category of all spontaneous, conscious human experience – it could even be called a 'synthetic *a priori* of human experience.' (Kant's description of the causal principle).[20] It binds human experience as a unity. It is the synthetic origin or ground undergirding human conscious experience.

There is therefore in such a manner an *original* 'revelation' of God to man, in what Schleiermacher terms God-consciousness, of the unmediated, immediate, spontaneous feeling of absolute dependence. But what must be noted is that what is given to us here is not God but a God-consciousness. Schleiermacher emphasises 'any possibility of God being given is entirely excluded because anything that is outwardly given must be given as an object exposed to our counter-influence, however slight this may be', and he adds 'the transference of the idea of God to any perceptible object, unless one is all the time conscious that it is a piece of purely arbitrary symbolism is always a corruption be it a temporary transference (*i.e.* theophany) or a constitutive transference in which God is represented as permanently a particular perceptible existence.'[21]

20. This is essentially the same point which A. I. C. Heron is making when he writes of Schleiermacher that 'this immediate consciousness of dependence is something which in Kantian language might be called "transcendental"'. *A Century of Protestant Theology*, p. 25.
21. *Ibid.*, §4, 4.

It only remains for Schleiermacher's purposes of offering a Christian apologetic to show that the feeling of absolute dependence is not only the most fundamental structure of man's experience but also the highest, most supreme moment of consciousness where, (adopting the thesis – antithesis – synthesis theme of the Romantic school) in a synthetic unity the antithesis between one individual and another vanishes in a form of consciousness which is not one of ourselves as individuals of a particular description but of ourselves as inseparably part of finite existence in general. Herein lies the essence of the Christian experience of communion which receives fullest expression in the common experience of our redemption by the man Jesus.

Comments on Schleiermacher's Approach – the Cartesian Character of his Apologetic

Descartes sought to prove the existence of God by a route of discovery within the self and its indubitable ideas and structures of thought. By way of the certainty of the *cogito ergo sum* he showed that inherent in man is an idea of infinitude which we can only ascribe to God. Schleiermacher's apologetic is reminiscent of this type of approach. The Enlightenment principle expressed in Pope's *Essays on Man* (1733-4) seems still to be working itself out in theology.

> Know then thyself, presume not God to scan,
> The proper study of Mankind is Man

Schleiermacher's Christian apologetics is saying in effect 'know yourself' (*gnothi seauton*) and you will discover the real essence of knowledge of God and thereby find the pure core of theological statement obscured beneath the layers of dogma. As Karl Barth points out, 'The great formal principle of Schleiermacher's theology is at the same time its material principle. Christian, pious self-awareness contemplates and describes itself: that is in principle the be-all and end-all of this theology.'[22]

The first question one feels compelled to ask is whether introspection is an adequate or trustworthy means of discovering the real nature of one's own Christian experience let alone the essence of the Christian faith.[23] Is it not the case that the true nature of the self and *a fortiori* of one's Christian faith and experience is irreducibly bipolar and inter-relational in character such that the Christian believer can only discover himself (and the true nature of his faith) in and through discovering the relationship to him of the God who is Other and yet who in personal love opens the eyes of the believer to discern his true self (and at the same time the truly relational character of faith) with the mind of Christ and with all the objectivity which accompanies this? Is this not, for the Christian, the only accurate and authentic path to knowledge of the self (and of the true nature of faith) and eminently more satisfactory as the way to self-knowledge than the attempt by the subject to turn his focus in upon himself (*incurvatus in se*) and thereby to delve analytically into the workings of his own feeling of absolute dependence – with all the philosophical problems which any such enterprise raises (see note 23). It is easy to be simplistic in one's criticism of

22. Karl Barth, *From Rousseau to Ritschl*, London, 1959, p. 338.
23. One must not forget the massive problems which both Hume and Kant found themselves confronting in their various attempts to expound the nature of self-identity. The former confesses, 'I cannot discover any theory which gives me satisfaction on this head.' *Treatise of Human Nature*, (ed. D. G. C. Macnabb, London, 1962), p. 331. Hume's method was doomed to fail since it is difficult to imagine how the self could receive a direct impression of that which is receiving the impressions! As Gilbert Ryle points out, in his *Concept of Mind*, the self which is the subject of introspection cannot simultaneously be the object of introspection. Indeed, it seems to me that this 'systematic elusiveness' of the 'I' in introspection can only cast doubt on the adequacy of any form of introspection as the proper way of self-discovery.

Schleiermacher but the following statement of Jurgen Moltmann seems to express something of the issue here:

> Of course the relationship between God and man is not a reciprocal relationship of causality and dependency either – if it is a relationship of covenant and love, then for man's experience of himself this question is not merely valid, it is necessary. Can a person experience 'himself' in his relationship to God as person if God is certainly supposed to mean everything to him but if he is not supposed to mean anything to God?[24]

This leads us to the further question as to whether Schleiermacher's apologetic results in a presentation of the Christian Faith which could itself give rise to the 'most supreme form of consciousness?' Is there not a danger of being parasitic here in that what is being advocated is a form of experience which can only result from believing more than this type of approach allows *i.e.* believing and trusting in a God who *is* given, self-giving? If God-consciousness is the 'given' of the Christian faith and not God, this would suggest that what would arise from his apologetic is not a God-consciousness but a 'God-consciousness'-consciousness which is not necessarily an experience of God at all.

Barth's Critique of Schleiermacher

Barth's criticisms are couched in the question as to how far Schleiermacher is ultimately true, as he wished to be, to the central tenets of the reformers. In Barth's eyes, Schleiermacher brought about a complete reversal in the order of thought of the reformers – a reversal which forces one to ask whether his formulation of the Christian faith can ultimately be described as 'reformed' dogmatics at all. Theology must work with the two ground-motifs God and man. But whereas the reformers represented this by way of their doctrines of the *Word of God* and *faith* as the hu-

---

24. J. Moltmann, *The Trinity and the Kingdom of God*, Eng. trans., London, 1981, pp. 3-4.

man correlate which at the same time is created through, sustained by and finds its basis in the Word of God, for Schleiermacher the centre of gravity moved from God to man such that in those places where the reformers had spoken of 'the Gospel' or 'the Word of God' or 'Christ', Schleiermacher, thinking in terms of man where the reformers had thought in terms of God, now speaks of 'religion' or 'piety' . The Copernican world-view prescribed and has now produced an anthropocentric theology.

Accordingly, the central theme of theology is not the out-pouring of the Holy Spirit but religious consciousness. Faith is no longer understood as God's revelation but as man's experience. Schleiermacher's apologetic concern has turned the Christian relationship of man to God into an apparently human possibility. Experience and history, corresponding to faith and Christ, are reconciled and brought together by way of a mediating relationship construed in terms of 'modes of cognition'.[25]

By contrast, in the writings of the reformers, Barth points out, 'the sole mediation which enters into consideration there is the recognition of the Father in the Son through the Spirit in the strict irreducible opposition of these persons in the Godhead. This mediation cannot be made comprehensible as a mode of human cognition. It is unusable in apologetics.[26] Schleiermacher's departure from the reformers by his reduction of faith in Christ to a mode of human cognition means finally that when he speaks of Christ and Christians and their mutual relationship what he actually has in mind is neither the one nor the other but one single concept embracing both, namely, 'the composite life', 'humanity', the 'history of human nature'. The importance of the Person of Christ is thereby reduced to the effectiveness of Christ on our feeling of absolute dependence. For it is this feeling of absolute dependence which functions as the cornerstone of the Christian religion and

25. K. Barth, *From Rousseau to Ritschl*, p. 344.
26. *Ibid.*, pp. 344-345.

not the Person of Christ. As Barth comments. 'According to the premisses of his concept of religion he was bound to renounce the idea of the Deity of Christ, or, to put it differently, to understand the Deity of Christ as the incomparable climax and decisive stimulator within the composite life of humanity.'[27]

Barth wrote a great deal on Schleiermacher[28] and one could discuss at length the various issues he raises and criticisms he makes. But what Barth sees is that firstly, Schleiermacher's apologetic concern, secondly, his Romantic concern for synthesis, for 'peace' and for harmony and thirdly, his dislike of intellectual dogmatic formulations led Schleiermacher to reinterpret out of Christianity the tension between our forms of life and the Word of God as it addresses us – that fundamental and necessary distinction between Christians and Christ, between what we are in ourselves and what we are in Christ and between the love and perfection of God on the one hand and the sinfulness of man on the other, which is the barrier to any 'natural' relation of man to God on man's part. As a result Schleiermacher not only fails to be true to the nature of Reformed Theology (which was his avowed concern) but also forces one to ask if he does not effect a *metabasis eis allo genos* (Kierkegaard) on the part of Christianity, that is, a transformation of Christianity into a religion of a completely different kind.

BARTH

In the light of Barth's criticisms of Schleiermacher and his profound awareness of the dangers of a Romantic or a Kantian approach to interpreting the role of experience in theology it is not surprising that Barth's main discussion of

27. *Ibid.*, p. 349.
28. Barth's own Schleiermacher lectures took an entire winter semester and in the English translation (*The Theology of Schleiermacher*, trans. G. W. Bromiley, Edinburgh, 1982) comprise nearly 300 pages.

experience comes in the first volume of his Church Dogmatics on the doctrine of the Word of God (Vol. 1, part 1). Barth's early experience in Marburg where theology was totally moulded by the Neo-Kantianism of Cohen and Natorp (the philosophy, incidentally, which as Roger Johnson has shown in his splendid book, *The Origins of Demythologising*, underlies and shapes Bultmann's entire theology and hermeneutic) showed him the extreme dangers of allocating religion to an independent realm of *non-cognitive* experience – what the Neo-Kantians had termed the realm of the *Individuum*. This home of religion was the sphere of unstructured experience as opposed to objective knowledge, of 'grace' (as they interpreted it) as opposed to 'law' – a purely subjective sphere devoid of any knowing or 'objectifying' activity. The Neo-Kantian approach like that of Schleiermacher could allow no room for understanding the God of Christianity as the God who gives himself to be known in Christ and where all Christian experience is thereby *cognitive* experience of God who is 'given' to us through his gracious act of self-accommodation to man. On Neo-Kantian presuppositions God is in no way 'given' for our knowing. The Neo-Kantians had therefore assigned religion to the sphere of *Erlebnis* and *Gefühl*, that is, forms of human experience which were defined as devoid of reason and of what they saw as objectifying intellectual activity. Schleiermacher's approach had let to similar conclusions. On both approaches the possibility of religion, religious experience and therefore of Christian faith was defined (indeed pre-determined) by the philosopher in terms of the conditions of experience, and capacities for it, discerned by him through introspective, subjective analysis and categorisation of the forms of human experience.

Robert Aboagye-Mensah has described in the following terms the resulting question facing Barth from 1915. 'If Christian theology takes its starting-point from the experience of faith and reflects on it then how does theology ever get beyond the subjectivism, relativism and anthropocentrism of this object of reflection? How can theology get beyond the subjectivity of faith to the objectivity of God as He is in Himself and his positive relationship to man and his societal structures? How can theology find a consistent basis for taking God rather than faith as the concrete reality from which theological concepts are derived? How can theory and Christian practice be consistently grounded, limited and orientated in terms of God's sovereignty alone?.[29]

It was in addressing this question that Barth's study of Anselm was so important. Theology is *fides quaerens intellectum*, faith seeking understanding in confronting God become man in Christ, the Word of God. It is of significance therefore that Barth's major discussion of experience is entitled 'The Word of God and Experience' and appears as one part of his section *The Knowability of the Word of God*.

Despite their disagreements on the nature of the knowledge of God two men, Brunner and Barth, sought to stand against the stream of prevailing thought and together set out to reassert that fundamental theological principle, which they had seen betrayed by so much religious thought. 'Through God alone can God be known.' In following this principle the latter saw clearly that if apologetics involves establishing, in advance of God's initiative in giving himself to be known, independent and prior capacities for knowledge of God (or 'modes of cognition' of God) on the part of finite and sinful human beings then there can be no Christian apologetic – since it cannot as such be a legitimate enterprise. The form as well as the content of experience of God is prescribed by the Word of God, God's self-communication. For far too long in the history of Christian thought the church had witnessed the struggle to find prior gaps in human knowledge and

---

29. R. K. Aboagye-Mensah, *The Socio-political Thinking of Karl Barth: Trinitarian and Incarnational Christology as the Ground for his Social Action and its Implications for us Today*, (unpublished Thesis, Aberdeen, 1984).

experience into which to fit man's knowledge and experience of God. As scientific knowledge has advanced through the centuries God was continually being brought in to prevailing scientific theories to act as the link and explanation in the various spaces or gaps in scientific knowledge and then being displaced when scientific explanation was given for the relevant gap. Similarly, in philosophy too God was continually 'on the move'! He first reigned as Lord in the sphere of reason and then, as this faculty and its speculative ideas were undermined by Hume and Kant, he was moved into the moral sphere as the postulate of moral action and moral experience. Schleiermacher moved him out of this realm due to his romantic distaste for moral dogmatism but then, a few decades later, Ritschl moved him back on account of the late nineteenth century distaste for Romanticism. Rudolf Otto created a new home for God in human experience through his postulation of the sense of the numinous and the Neo-Kantians finally established God in the realm of non-cognitive *Erlebnis* and *Gefühl* which was finally to become, in Bultmann, man's existential openness to the unknown or 'faith'.

Barth set out to spell the end of this (Kantian) attempt to see God as a postulate of some venerated (or usually simply fashionable) form of human experience since on this approach man established himself as Lord over God's revelation whereas, as Barth affirms on page one of the Church Dogmatics 'God is the Lord from whom and to whom we exist.'[30] God reveals himself as Lord over all forms of human knowledge and experience and this revelation is the Word of God which 'can become intelligible only in terms of itself'. As a result, the task of apologetics is in effect redefined in terms of the Proclamation of the Word of God where God's Word is the Triune God himself

---

30. K. Barth, *Church Dogmatics* Vol. 1 Part 1, Eng. Trans., Edinburgh, 1978, p. 187.

in his revelation as Revealer, Revelation and Revealedness.

One might say that, if Schleiermacher had echoed the Copernican revolution in the sciences through which man became the centre of the universe, the anthropocentrism inherent in this was redressed by an 'Einsteinian revolution' whereby the object of knowledge and investigation was now given priority and seen as interpreting itself in its own essential structures and in all its objectivity by conditioning, prescribing and bringing into conformity with itself the scientist's modes of research. God is now, for Barth, to be understood as he interprets himself by grace in his own Being and internal relations to man demanding of the theologian reverence, obedience and 'wonder' whereby God as the Supreme Reality moulds and shapes our knowing processes through the Holy Spirit that they might by Grace come to be open, despite their fallibility, to God's self-accommodation.

At the beginning of his discussion of *The Word of God and Experience,* Barth reminds us of his definition of knowledge as 'the confirmation of human acquaintance with an object whereby its truth becomes a determination of the existence of the man who has the knowledge'. He then adds, 'the determination of the man who has the knowledge we call experience.'[31] Here we find the beginning *firstly* of a *holistic* conception of experience and secondly of a radically *bipolar* (as opposed to unipolar) conception of experience. Experience is not a special category of some non-cognitive, pseudo-form of knowledge of God as it was for Schleiermacher, the Neo-Kantians and also for Bultmann; experience is rather the unitary determination of the whole man through his being confronted by the Truth that lies beyond him, by God's Word. Barth stresses that any determination of human existence by God's Word is not to be confused with a determination man can give his existence. This experience cannot be conceived as a

---

31. *Ibid.,* p. 198.

cooperation between divine determining and human self-determining nor as resulting from a simultaneity or interrelation with regard to these. In Barth's words, 'if man lets himself be told by the Word of God that he has a Lord, that he is the creature of this Lord, that he is a lost sinner blessed by Him, that he awaits eternal redemption and is thus a stranger in this sphere of time, this specific content of the Word experienced by him will flatly prohibit him from ascribing the possibility of this experience to himself either wholly or in part or from dialectically equating the divine possibility actualised in this experience with a possibility of his own.'[32] Any attempt to argue for a mutual involvement or interrelation here could only be advocated by an external onlooker who failed to realise that 'the co-existence of God and man as it occurs in the experience of God's Word is not a co-existence on the same level, so that it is completely impossible to see it from a higher vantage point and to view it in its possibility.'[33] The approach of the external onlooker who fails to grasp 'the self-knowledge of man in real experience of God's Word as we know it from the biblical promise'[34] also overlooks the fact that 'there can be no point in trying to maintain man's self-determination in some way, even dialectically, over against the determination of man by God. Precisely as self-determination, it is subject to determination by God. Our very self-determination needs this determination by God in order to be experience of His Word.'[35]

There is therefore no possibility of supplanting the determination of man by God with self-determination, as Pelagius wished, or with a theory of cooperation, as the semi-Pelagians wished, or of describing the forms of determination as identical as Augustine wished. Barth hereby avoids anthropomorphism. In Karl Rahner's phrase

32. *Ibid.*, p. 199
33. *Ibid.*, p. 200.
34. *Ibid.*, p. 199.
35. *Ibid.*, p. 200.

'God is not part of the furniture of the world', and he cannot be regarded as such when we seek to formulate a proper understanding of our experience of him. Secondly, for Barth, Christian experience is radically objective, responsive and bipolar such that it will not have a form separate from the Biblical conception of Christian love as responsive, objective, initiated by God and sustained by the Holy Spirit. Accordingly, in his exposition of the nature of Christian experience, he seeks not only to be true to Scripture and to the nature of faith but also to reflect a unitary and holistic understanding of man in relation to his Creator.

Despite his emphasis on God's determination of ourselves in any experience that we might have which can truly be said to be an *experience of God*, Barth is also emphatic that this does not mean an elimination of man's self-determination or a view of man as existing in a state of partial or total receptivity or passivity. For this reason he rejects Schleiermacher's term *dependence*. The nature of the encounter between God and man is such that, 'If God is seriously involved in experience of the Word of God then man is just as seriously involved too.' He continues: 'the very man who stands in real knowledge of the Word of God also knows himself as existing in the act of his life, as existing in his self-determination.'[36] Barth's point is however that our very self-determination needs determination by God in order to be experience of his Word. 'If human self-determination were not as it were the material which is subject and in need when we speak of the determination of human existence by the Word of God, then how could we speak of the determination of human existence or indeed of a determination by God's Word in any sense?'[37] Man's self-determination receives direction, is set under judgement and has impressed upon it a character by the

---

36. *Ibid.*, p. 200.
37. *Ibid.*, p. 201.

Word of God. The very word *Word* implies such a determining of experience, such a directing on the part of God.

Barth now goes on to argue that, on the basis of what has been said, it can be seen to be mistaken to emphasise any one anthropological locus of experience of God, *e.g.* will or conscience or feeling. Theological systems have been built on one or the other and, as I suggested above, as fashions change, so the emphasis moves from one to another. Schleiermacher's system was rooted in feeling conceived in a certain manner. Ritschl, under the influence of Kant's moral theology, saw moral experience as the home of experience of God and so the moral conscience was given primary place in religious experience. Barth on the other hand refuses to have any fashion-dictated human home for experience of God and writes, 'We may quietly regard the will and conscience and feeling and all other possible anthropological centres as possibilities of human self-determination and then understand them in their totality as determined by the Word of God which affects the whole man.'[38]

This brings us to the second point which is in effect the negative side of his first. He also sees no reason to invest certain anthropological centres with the fundamental distrust and suspicion that is often found in the history of theology. He has especially in mind the recurring fashion to wage war against the so-called 'intellect' of man, his powers of thought and understanding, as the locus of possible religious experience of the Word of God. He sees two directly opposite reasons advanced for the special incompetence of the intellect in matters of religious experience. One group sees the intellect in this area as driving man back into the indolent passivity of mere reflection and contemplation whereas the other sees the activity of the intellect as representing an overbold self-determination which ought to be broken in experience of the Word of God. On one view the intellect lacks the real power and on

38. *Ibid.*, p. 202.

the other view it lacks the real humility, and on both the real depth that one hopes to encounter at other anthropological centres e.g. conscience or feeling, as distinct from the intellect.[39]

Where therefore does the emphasis in Barth lie? His concern is to stress the following: firstly, experience of the Word of God takes place in the Spirit and is irreducibly *personal* – it is certainly not, as some have argued,[40] simply the detached, intellectual assent to some body of truths; it is a personal encounter with the Person of God. As Barth himself stressed 'we, too, see no reason anthropologically to prefer the intellect especially.'[41] Secondly, there can be no emphasis on one anthropological locus of Christian faith at the cost of any other since all human encounter with the Word of God is a unitary and all-embracing, personal experience of God. But for precisely this reason Barth is also concerned that by way of reaction against any cold rationalism we do not over-react and

---

39. *Ibid.*, p. 202.
40. The suspicion that Barth is guilty of placing too weighty an emphasis on the 'intellect ' of man is reflected in the pamphlet publicising the 1984 FEET Conference where it suggests that Barth places too much emphasis on 'purely intellectual assent' to a set of doctrines at the cost of playing down 'Christian experience in the power of the Holy Spirit'. At another point it comments, 'In this post-Barthian era, however, the questions of the 19th century, largely ignored by Barth, have come back with a vengeance. Contemporary theology is again dominated by the question: What is the relationship between revelation and experience?' However precisely the opposite fear amongst other groups of evangelical theologians is also a source of vehement criticism of Barth. As Professor G. W. Bromiley (a translator/editor of the English translation of Barth and the person who communicated to Barth the criticisms of him made by van Til, Clark and Klooster et al.) comments: 'the notion that Barth is simply a theologian of experience (basically a follower of Schleiermacher !) . . . still lingers in many circles.' (G. W. Bromiley, *Introduction to the Theology of Karl Barth*, Edinburgh, 1979, p. 10.
41. *Church Dogmatics* 1, 1, p. 202.

thereby limit personal experience of the Word of God simply to the experience of feeling. Barth's overriding concern is that we do not restrict the possibility of the experience of God's Word at *any* point. Any such restriction can only ultimately involve a complete denial of it. But, to the extent that God's Word is spoken to man, 'experience of it must at least include also the intellect, and the claiming of the intellect' and, he emphasises, 'the Word of God that determines human existence is strong enough to deal also with man as he determines himself in thought.' The restriction of the experience of the Word of God in any direction must be regarded as 'a form of cramp from which one must be healed to be able to see what is really to be seen here'.[42]

To summarise Barth's thesis in his own words, 'From different angles the determination of human existence by God's Word can be understood just as much as a determination of feeling, will, or intellect, and psychologically it may actually be more the one than the other in a given case. The decisive point materially, however, is that it is a determination of the whole self-determining man.'[43]

We now come to the question in what the experience of God's Word (*i.e.* the determination of the whole self-determining man by God's Word) might then consist. The introductory thesis to Barth's lengthy discussion of 'The Knowability of the Word of God' runs as follows, echoing the concern which, in his criticism of Schleiermacher, he emphasised as being central to the approach of the reformers: 'The reality of the Word of God in all its three forms is grounded only in itself. So, too, the knowledge of it by men can consist only in its acknowledgement, and this acknowledgement can become real only through itself and can become intelligible only in terms of itself.'[44]

---

42. *Ibid.*, p. 203.
43. *Ibid.*, p. 204.
44. *Ibid.*, p. 187.

Barth describes the specific character of experience of the Word of God therefore as *acknowledgement* construed in the following terms:

(1). The word acknowledgement entails first the concept of knowledge. This is so since the Word of God is primarily and predominantly *speech*, communication from person to person, the Word of truth.

(2). Experience as acknowledgement is personal and relational, involving a relation of man as person to another person, naturally the person of God.

(3). Acknowledgement relates to a definite control with respect to the one who acknowledges. Acknowledgement of God's Word by man consists of avowal of and submission to the purposes of God declared in God's Word.

(4). Acknowledgement of God's Word means respect for the fact that takes place in God's Word – in particular its coming to us as revelation, Holy Scripture and Church proclamation.

(5). To have experience of God is to yield to his supremacy. Acknowledgement of the Word of God arises in a context of obedience and submission between those who are utterly unequal. Experience of God's Word therefore bends man and brings him into conformity with itself.

(6). Acknowledgement means decision. The coming of God's Word to man is the act of divine freedom and choice. It comes according to God's good pleasure and it is again God's good-pleasure how it comes to him, whether for grace or judgement. Experience of the Word of God is experience of the divine freedom and choice, and therefore it is itself decision, decision concerning man which is manifested as the characterising of man's decision as a decision for faith or unbelief, for obedience or disobedience.

(7). Acknowledgement points to the fact that man is halting before an enigma standing in a situation which is not open but which is unexplained from the standpoint of the person who does the acknowledging. Deep within the experience of the Word of God therefore lies respect for the mystery of this Word that man acknowledges.

(8). Experience as a form of acknowledgement is not passive but dynamic. It denotes an act or movement on man's part. The experience of the God who encounters us can never be considered an attitude, therefore this movement cannot be arrested by any *synthesis* on man's part. It is within this movement that a man acknowledges the mystery of the Word of God and has Christian experience.

(9). In acknowledgement man submits to the authority of the other. In the act of acknowledgement, the life of man, without ceasing to be the self-determining life of this man, has now its centre, its whence, the meaning of its attitude, and the criterion whether this attitude really has the corresponding meaning – it has all this outside itself, in the Word of God acknowledged in and through Christian experience.[45]

By way of this conception of the nature of Christian experience Barth seeks to put an end to all forms of what he calls 'Christian Cartesianism' – the notion that somehow we can be responsible for the immanence of the possibility of experience of God's Word, the notion that we can 'put our hand in the fire for it'. The new man in Christ cannot assert that his Christian experience is anything other than a total experience of God in all his Grace and personal, self-revealing 'objectivity' – an experience wrought in him by that same God. There is no possibility of any part of Saul working on Saul to produce Paul. The conversion of Saul was a total regeneration (*metanoia*) and determination by God of Saul's whole framework of experience such that neither Paul nor Saul could find any element of Paul's Christian experience in Saul.[46] Paul could only describe himself in terms of his relationship to God, or rather God's relationship with him,[47] and therefore no Christian experi-

---

45. *Ibid.*, pp. 205-208.
46. Similarly, as von Balthasar points out in his book *On Prayer*, only Peter and not Simon could have discerned God's mission for him and only the Peter in Simon Peter could have confessed, 'Thou art the Christ.'
47. *Cf.* Gal. 2:20. 'It is no longer I who live but Christ who lives in me.' And note also the self-correction in Gal. 4:9. 'now that you have come to know God, or rather to be known by God . . .'.

ence could be described in any other terms than in the bipolar terms of total, personal experience of Christ, the Word made flesh. 'When the Word of God is present to us, this means that we are turned away from ourselves and towards the Word of God, that we are orientated to it'. This is the essence of new life in Christ and all the experiences which accompany it.

Conclusion

The point has been made that Barth's theological emphases have not always reflected enough the variety of areas of human experience in the context of which God comes to man. His conception of Christian experience seems predominantly to be a joyful and optimistic one which is reflected perhaps in Barth's at times almost embarrassingly extravagant praise and adulation of the music of Mozart. As a result, one feels compelled to ask whether this does not reflect the fact that, although Barth suffered family tragedy on more than one occasion, he did not seem to have to face guilt, or national shame, or the humiliation of his cause in the same way that, for example, a theologian like Jürgen Moltmann had to.[48] As a result Moltmann seems to be able to express the Christian experience of God within the depths of guilt, of despair, of disillusionment and of hopelessness in a more profound and human way than Barth could have. One suspects that Barth's theology would perhaps have been enriched if he had been able to appreciate equally fully the music of Beethoven or Brahms or perhaps even Rachmaninoff in addition to that of Mozart! All human experience of God is bipolar and the psychological character and subjective context of human experience of the Word of God is something which God himself takes into account in his self-accommodation to man. Therefore the character of Christ's life on earth and of his death on the cross, his suffering, his awareness of be-

---

48. See his essay, 'Why am I a Christian?', in *Experiences of God*, Eng. trans., London, 1980.

ing despised reveal God's identification with elements of human experience which must mean that the *logic* of Christian experience of the Word of God which Barth has portrayed so brilliantly must be seen to take on a variety of forms and be present in different contexts of man's experience of God.

This brings us finally to a point which may help us to respond positively to the concerns of those who see Barth as playing down the distinctively human side of Christian experience. In response to this I would suggest that one should distinguish perhaps between *Christian experience* as the structure of man's unitary and total determination by God in his self revelation and *the experiences of the Christian* in this context. Christian experience may arise from God's meeting man in a variety of different contexts of guilt, or suffering, of forsakenness and so on, and similarly Christian experience may give rise to a variety of different experiences on the part of the subject. *Christian experience* on this model refers to the nature of the relationship between God and man which Barth delineated whereas the *Christian experiences* refer to the human subjective pole in this relationship and the character of the context addressed by God and the response to this address. Barth could be said therefore not to have focussed attention fully enough on the latter. But our response must surely not be to reject Barth's analysis of the structure of Christian experience as construed in terms of the Word of God's dynamic relationship to the whole man and as worked out through confronting 'calls from the caves' which still echo and haunt us today. Rather our response must be to focus on the fundamental nature and character of Christian experience that is *truly* experience of the Word of God. At the same time, however, we must also realise the diversity of contexts in which this takes place and the manner in which they are used richly by God in the profoundly human depths of God's self-communication to man and thereby avoid constricting, in theological exposition, the forms of expression of man's subjective enjoyment and celebration of God's gracious self-gift as it is encountered in the dynamic Christian experience of the Word of God.

THE ROLE OF EXPERIENCE IN CHRISTIAN THEOLOGY SINCE BARTH

CHRISTINA A. BAXTER

Recent theology has circled round the question of the role of religious experience and the problems associated with it, without offering or reaching definitive answers. This paper attempts to focus some of the key questions in this area, by showing how some theologians are tackling the issues.

Are there Religious Experiences?

The prime question is whether there is anything which may fairly be called religious experience. At the popular level, the mechanical view of the universe assumes that in principle everything is explicable in terms of its material components,[1] lending credence to the anthropological, social, and psychological 'explanations' of the idea and experience of God offered by Feuerbach, Marx and Freud.[2] But at the deeper level of research and investigation, contemporary science is offering a vastly different understanding of a reality that is not closed or predetermined.[3] This offers not only a more congenial atmosphere in which to make claims to religious experience and revelation, but also the opportunity to construct a fresh epistemology in which decisions in favour of the existence and experience of God are at least as plausible as those against. Hans Küng has argued in this kind of way in his massive answer to the question: 'Does God exist?'[4]

1. See further A. R. Peacocke, *Creation and the World of Science*, Oxford, 1979, pp. 52-55.
2. See further H. Küng, *Does God Exist?*, London, 1980, pp. 189-339.
3. See further A. R. Peacocke, *op. cit.*, p. 55-63.
4. He concludes: '. . . the question "Does God exist?" can now be answered by a clear convinced Yes, justifiable at the bar of critical reason.' H. Küng *op. cit.*, p. 702.

EXPERIENCE IN CHRISTIAN THEOLOGY SINCE BARTH

While theological and philosophical debate about the possibility of religious experience continued, others turned their attention to the question in a fresh way. Some have investigated the religious experiences of mankind for what they claim to be,[5] but others have taken a phenomenological attitude, deliberately 'bracketing out' questions of whether there is anything giving rise to the experience, and focussing entirely on the way religious experiences manifest themselves in human behaviour.[6] But both methods recognise that there is something here which is worthy of investigation, and both methods make available more classified material with which to answer questions about the origin, interpretation and reality of religious experience.[7] For example, Mircea Eliade, writing in 1956 comments on the encounter between modern and traditional mentalities which has occurred as western studies have increasingly explored eastern and primitive religions. He considers that '. . . the meeting and confrontation of these two types of civilisation count amongst the most significant events of the last quarter of a century.'[8] His book *Myths, Dreams and Mysteries* in which this assessment occurs, describes religious experiences in primitive cultures, and it is an area which has been studied by E. Durkheim,[9] G. van der Leeuw,[10] N. Smart and others.[11]

5. *E.g.* Religious Experience Research Unit, Manchester College, Oxford, which has produced several publications. *E.g.* E. Robinson, *The Original Vision, A Study of the Religious Experience of Childhood*, Oxford, 1977.
6. *E.g.* N. Smart, *The Phenomenon of Religion*, London, 1978.
7. For a discussion of this see W. Pannenberg, *Basic Questions in Theology* II, London, 1971, pp. 65-118.
8. M. Eliade, *Myths, Dreams and Mysteries*, London, 1970, p. 9.
9. E. Durkheim, *The Elementary Forms of the Religious Life*, New York, 1965).
10. G. van der Leeuw, *Religion in Essence and Manifestation: A Study in Phenomenology*, London and Gloucester, Mass., 1938.
11. N. Smart, *The Religious Experiences of Mankind*, London, 1971. For a bibliography of other classic works see N. Smart, *op. cit.*, pp. 701-705, and Kenneth Wilson 'Bibliography:

Such investigation grew out of earlier work which had less sociological, psychological and phenomenological precision.[12]

This academic study, beginning before our period, has become of increasing significance in an age where plurality of religious experience is no longer a remote curiosity, but a close encounter, at least in Great Britain, where Sikh temples and Muslim mosques have become part of the western landscape. Contemporary man, with all the benefits of mass communication, is well aware that whilst there may be 'only one earth'[13] there are certainly many world views.[14] In Britain, it has become possible to study world religions in degree courses, and it is part of the religious education syllabus in many schools. University courses in phenomenology of religion and comparative religion or school courses on Buddhism, Hinduism, and Sikhism may seem far removed from Christian academic theology, but this confrontation of civilisations, world views, and religions has forced Christian theologians to handle the questions thrown up by the acknowledged plurality of experience and interpretation in a more thorough-going and sophisticated way than Barth and his contemporaries ever attempted. Consequently we find both Catholic and Protestant theologians attempting to come to terms with these phenomena. We will look briefly at examples of this.

Are All Religions Experiencing the Same God?
Karl Rahner, facing the continued existence of other religions after two thousand years of Christian mission,[15] in

---

Religious and Scientific Experience', *Modern Churchman* 26, 1983, pp. 48-52.
12. *E.g.* R. Otto, *The Idea of the Holy*, Oxford, 1923.
13. Title of a book by B. Ward and R. Dubos, Harmondsworth, 1972.
14. For a discussion of this see P. Berger, *The Social Reality of Religion*, pp. 1-60.
15. K. Rahner, 'Christianity and the Non-Christian Religions', in *Theological Investigations* V, London, 1966, pp. 115-134.

which it has been constantly claimed that 'it is *the* religion, the one and only valid revelation of the one living God...'[16] suggests that 'the question about the understanding of and continued existence of religious pluralism as a factor in our immediate Christian existence is an urgent one...'[17] While maintaining the absolute claim to truth for Christianity as unique, Rahner argues beyond traditional Catholic affirmation of the natural knowledge of God available to all through rational reflection on the world. On the basis of his belief in God's universal salvific intentions,[18] he suggests that 'every human being is really and truly exposed to the influence of divine, supernatural grace which offers an interior union with God and by means of which God communicates himself whether the individual takes up an attitude of acceptance or refusal towards this grace.'[19] Indeed, man is 'orientated by grace towards the immediacy of God in a dimension of *a priori* awareness',[20] and finds himself faced with 'the creative call of infinite mystery'.[21] Where there is response to this offer, Rahner asserts it is appropriate to describe the individuals concerned as 'anonymous Christians': anonymous because they have not yet understood what they have responded to, nor openly confessed their implicit faith; Christian because God's offer of saving grace can only be that won for all by Christ at Calvary.[22] But 'an individual can already be in possession of sanctifying grace, can in other words be justified and sanctified, as a child of God, an heir to heaven, positively orientated

16. K. Rahner, *op. cit.*, p. 116
17. K. Rahner, *Op. cit.*, p. 117.
18. *E.g.* K. Rahner, 'Anonymous Christians' in *Theological Investigations VI*, London, 1969, p. 391.
19. K. Rahner, 'Christianity and the non-Christian Religions', *op. cit.*, p. 123.
20. K. Rahner, 'Observations on the Problem of the "Anonymous Christian"', in *Theological Investigations* XIV, London, 1979, p. 289.
21. K. Rahner, 'Anonymous Christians', *op.cit.*, p. 392.
22. K. Rahner, 'Christianity and Non-Christian Religions', *op.cit.*, p. 122.

by grace towards his supernatural and eternal salvation even before he has explicitly embraced a credal statement of the Christian faith and been baptised. What 'anonymous Christianity' signifies first and foremost is that interior grace which forgives man and gives him a share in the Godhead even before baptism.'[23] Rahner offers two pictures of this: the first the seed of faith growing secretly to fruition in open Christian confession;[24] the second the gradual progress up the ladder to full church membership which begins in anonymity, proceeding through baptism and justification to sanctification as full eucharistic members of the body of Christ.[25]

Outside of the Christian church, Rahner considers that 'in a great many cases at least, grace gains the victory in man's free acceptance of it',[26] but because individuals are part of society, they express this religious experience through the religion of their time and place, whilst retaining the privilege of making reforming contributions to it.[27] These religions are therefore permitted as legitimate by God until the gospel is made known to them. Consequently 'there are supernatural grace-filled elements in non-christian religions',[28] but this by no means guarantees that they are not erroneous.

Rahner suggests that his view that saving experience of God is available outside the Church in other religions or in atheism[29] is not only compatible with early Catholic dogma, but required by Christian doctrines of God and man

23. K. Rahner, 'Anonymous Christianity and the Missionary Task of the Church', in *Theological Investigations* XII, London, 1974, p. 165.
24. K. Rahner, 'Observations on the Problem of the "Anonymous Christian"', *Op. cit.*, p. 29
25. K. Rahner, 'Anonymous Christians', *op. cit.*, p. 391.
26. K. Rahner, 'Christianity and the non-Christian Religions', *op.cit.*, p. 124.
27. *Ibid.*, p. 129.
28. *Ibid.*, p. 121.
29. K. Rahner 'Observations on the Problem of the "Anonymous Christian"', *op.cit.*, p. 28.

especially after the decisions taken by Vatican II.[30] Christianity, he affirms, 'believes that God can be victorious by his secret grace even when the Church does not win the victory.'[31]

Hans Küng does not find this attempt to handle the religious experiences of mankind satisfactory. 'Is not the whole of good-willed humanity thus swept with an elegant gesture across the paper-thin bridge of a theological fabrication into the back door of the "Holy Roman Church", leaving no one of goodwill "outside"?'[32] He suggests that it is a semantical exercise which redefines 'church' and 'salvation', whilst ignoring the fact that many of the 'anonymous Christians' do not want to be included in this way. Such a solution excludes the possibility of genuine dialogue with other religions because it does not respect the claim of the outsider to be different. Such dialogue, Küng considers imperative.

However, Küng would want to affirm that 'there is salvation outside the Church',[33] which he sees as a radical departure made by Vatican II from the earlier Catholic position.[34] Moreover, he would suggest that even though 'all men − even in the world religions − can be saved, this certainly does not mean that all religions are equally true'.[35] What must be said is that despite their variety, all religions have 'a genuine spiritual experience of the Absolute. . . .'[36] He continues: 'but the agreement must not be simplified, the differences must not be smoothed out, the utterly ambiguous inward religious experience must

30. *Cf.*, K. Rahner, 'Anonymous Christians', *op.cit.*, p. 397; K. Rahner 'Anonymous Christianity and the Missionary Task of the Church', *op.cit.*, p. 165ff.; K. Rahner, 'Observations on the Problem of the "Anonymous Christian"', *op. cit.*, p. 284-290.
31. K. Rahner, 'Christianity and the Non-Christian Religions', *op. cit.*, p. 134.
32. H. Küng, *On Being a Christian*, London, 1980, p. 98.
33. *Ibid.*, p. 91.
34. *Ibid.*, p. 97.
35. *Ibid.*, p. 104.
36. *Ibid.*, p. 102.

not be made absolute, as if all religious statements that can be articulated ... were irrelevant by comparison with this inward religious experience.'[37] Nevertheless, his discussion of the ideas of God found in different religions makes it clear that both inside and outside of Christianity knowledge about God and experience of him are possible.[38] The transcendent-immanent God is 'infinitely distant and yet closer to us than we are ourselves; not perceptible even when his presence is experienced; present even when his absence is experienced.[39] Indeed, the genuine open dialogue between the religions which he advocates must never forget that 'it is a question *more of human beings* and their living experiences *than merely of concepts, ideas or systems* ...' because religions 'are living faiths which are constantly freshly experienced by real men ...'[40] [41] There must thus be mutual criticism and enrichment which never falls into syncretism or admits exclusive claims of dominance. Christianity is unique, Küng believes, but must relate as a servant to other faiths.

J. Moltmann offers a Protestant attempt to reflect on the religious experiences claimed by non-Christian faiths. He has a section on 'Christianity and the World Religions' in his book *The Church in the Power of the Spirit*.[42] Characteristically, he approaches the problem from a dynamic and eschatological perspective, contrasting the separate religious histories of the past with the emergence of a single global future: 'the future of the nations is a single humanity'.[43] Henceforth, Christian theologians cannot regard other religions and their experiences as either 'enemies or superstitions from which Christianity ... freed

37. *Ibid.*, p. 102f.
38. H. Küng, *Does God Exist?*, London, 1980, pp.600ff.
39. *Ibid.*, p. 602.
40. H. Küng, *On Being a Christian*, p. 115.
41. *Ibid.*, p. 111f.
42. J. Moltmann, *The Church in the Power of the Spirit*, London, 1977, pp. 150-163.
43. *Ibid.*, p. 151.

men and women'.⁴⁴ There must be dialogue and co-operation, whether Christians speak from positions of strength or weakness. Although he does not rule out the possibility of traditional mission, which brings people to acknowledge the lordship of Christ, he suggests that 'mission has another goal as well';⁴⁵ that of influencing those with no Christian allegiance. Through dialogue 'the whole atmosphere of life'⁴⁶ can be changed so that pressing social problems can be tackled together. In dialogue Christians must make themselves vulnerable, open to change. 'Fruitful dialogue involves clear knowledge about the identity of one's own faith on the one hand, but on the other it requires a feeling of one's own incompleteness and a real sense of need for fellowship with the other.'⁴⁷

Moltmann believes that the significant Christian contribution to this dialogue will include emphasis on hope and liberation which will give to other faiths a 'messianic direction towards the kingdom'.⁴⁸ Agreeing generally with Küng against syncretistic and dominance models of relationship, he asserts: 'What is at issue is the charismatic quickening of different religious gifts, powers and potentialities for the kingdom of God and the liberation of men',⁴⁹ but he recognises that this dialogue is in 'its first modest and hesitant beginnings'.⁵⁰

W. Pannenberg comes to similar conclusions about the way in which non-Christian religious experience should be assessed, but for substantially different reasons.⁵¹ Pannenberg's reaction against the theories of history held by his Protestant theological predecessors is well known,

44. *Ibid.*, p. 151.
45. *Ibid.*, p. 152.
46. *Ibid.*, p. 152.
47. *Ibid.*, p. 159.
48. *Ibid.*, p. 163.
49. *Ibid.*, p. 163.
50. *Ibid.*, p. 159.
51. W. Pannenberg, *Basic Questions in Theology II*, London, 1971, pp. 65-118.

and his theory about religious experience fits neatly into his framework of thought in which God is known throughout all history which is open to the future, but especially and proleptically in Christ.[52] Recognising that a religious experience may be a separate event, Pannenberg nevertheless affirms that 'religious experiences do not possess such self-evidence as isolated events, but by their reference to the whole current experience of existence'.[53] Thus the single event needs to be interpreted in the light of all events, as the single event can shed light on the other events. In this way the infinite is perceived through and beyond a series of finite experiences. Pannenberg draws an interesting contrast between the Judaeo-Christian interpretation of religious experience, and that of other traditions. Whereas Israel related these experiences in hope to a greater future, and in a way which was open to re-interpretation and transformation, the myths of the religions are related to primordial times. But, Pannenberg suggests, 'the presence of provisional fulfilments of the divine mystery is experienced in every human life'.[54] Consequently, he too holds that religious experience outside of Judaeo-Christianity is experience of the God and Father of our Lord Jesus Christ. 'The alien religions cannot be adequately interpreted as mere fabrications of man's strivings after the true God. Ultimately, they have to do with the same divine reality as the message of Jesus'.[55] Radical differences in interpreting these experiences of the same God have occurred because other religions have confused the infinite with the finite, and have static temporal views of God.[56]

---

52. See W. Pannenberg (ed.). *Revelation as History*, London, 1969.
53. W. Pannenberg, *Basic Questions in Theology* II, p. 104.
54. *Ibid*, p. 104.
55. *Ibid.*, p. 115.
56. *Ibid.*, p. 115.

EXPERIENCE IN CHRISTIAN THEOLOGY SINCE BARTH

What is Religious Experience?

If the prime question of this area of contemporary theology is whether there is such a thing as religious experience, the second question is whether all religions bear witness to the phenomenon in their talk of religious experience. Beyond that, of course one would need to investigate, thirdly, whether there is any reality or realities outside of this universe which give rise to that experience. Although it would seem that the second question begs the answer to the first, it may in fact be the case that the answer to the first question depends on the resolution of the second. It would be hard to discover whether there is such a thing as indigestion until one had some kind of definition of what indigestion is, so that one might devise tests for it. But of course it is only as individuals experience indigestion that we are able to compare case with case to establish whether we are dealing with one phenomenon or several.

When we attempt this classification with religious experience we are faced with a plethora of possibilities. Indeed this paper would have been easier to write if one could be sure that authors were all referring to the same thing when they used the term 'religious experience'. Perhaps a general classification will help. First, there is a very wide view of religious experience which holds that in principle all experiences may be received religiously and therefore all are potentially religious. A. Kee asserts the opposite, that 'there are no direct experiences of God, only experiences which are interpreted in a religious manner'.[57] There is a distinction to be made between those who would urge that any experience could be interpreted religiously, and those who suggest any experience might be so received or interpreted, but not all in fact either are or should be. This latter position is held by M. Thornton, an Anglican specialist in ascetical theology, who argues that the universal ordinariness of religious experience is the

---

57. A Kee, *The Way of Transcendence*, London, 1971, p. 18.

necessary corollary of God's omnipresence,[58] although it is God's choice when and where religious experiences occur.[59]

Thirdly, there are those who would not see either all events or some events as religious experience, but rather would understand it in terms of encounter. For example, Jean Mouroux, a Roman Catholic theologian who has written an extensive study of the subject, defines religion as 'fundamentally a personal relationship to God'[60] and religious experience as 'the act - or group of acts - through which man becomes aware of himself in relation to God.'[61] M. Eliade describes how encounter may come through sensible things which may be quite ordinary[62] as well as through things set apart to be sacred. Mouroux would admit that this encounter can be through sensible things, but he would add that it could also be through the intellect, through the emotions or through spiritual feeling.

In cataloguing those who understand experience in terms of encounter one is forced to ask whether there should be a differentiation between those who believe God can be encountered through events or things and those who believe that he may be encountered through Scripture. Theologians who view Scripture through existentialist spectacles, and claim to encounter Jesus through the Word written or preached do not always make it clear why they would regard this as revelation rather than religious experience. Indeed, those who would hold that the written record itself is revelation need to give some thought to this distinction, lest they find that they have simply made one man's religious experience, the next man's revelation.

58. M. Thornton, *My God. A Reappraisal of Normal Religious Experience*, London, 1974, p. 15.
59. *Ibid.*, p. 46.
60. J. Mouroux, *The Christian Experience*, London, 1955.
61. *Ibid.*, p. 15.
62. M. Eliade, *Myths, Dreams and Mysteries*, London, 1970, pp. 72-98.

Finally there are those who see religious experience as primarily to be found through the experience of being human. This is close to Schleiermacher's view that 'religion is essentially contemplative':[63] the religious man is the one who feels:[64] 'to feel, that is to say, that our being and living is a being and living in and through God'.[65] Rahner describes religious experience in similar terms: man in experiencing his freedom, openness and transcendence 'already experiences the offer of grace...,[66] indeed the gospel of grace makes explicit 'what man already experiences implicitly in the depth of his being.'[67]

It will be appreciated that whilst there are differences as to how religious experience may be described, there are bound to be debates about what part religious experience plays in Christian life and theology. It is to these two areas that we must now turn.

The Part of Religious Experience in the Christian Life

This section depends chiefly on three books which have given systematic treatment to this matter: H. D. Lewis' *Our Experience of God*, Jean Moroux's *The Christian Experience*, and M. Thornton's *My God*. They attempt to answer the thorny questions which face us in this area.

All three authors are agreed about the importance of religious experience. Lewis suggests that 'the core of religion is religious experience'.[68] and, arguing against those who would hold that revelation should have this primacy, he says 'it seems highly artificial to suppose that God works primarily in the world through "given images" and

---

63. F. Schleiermacher, *On Religion: Speeches to its Cultured Despisers*, New York, 1958, p. 36.
64. *Ibid.*, p. 57: 'if you imagine it [religion] implanted in man quite alone ... he would only feel.'
65. *Ibid.*, p. 50.
66. K. Rahner, 'Anonymous Christians', *op.cit.*, p. 394.
67. *Ibid.*, p. 394.
68. H. D. Lewis, *Our Experience of God*, London, 1970, p. 72.

not more directly in the very substance of living'.⁶⁹ Questions of primacy or centrality are notoriously difficult: the weight or order in which any individual may assess the matter may be immaterial to serious theological reflection, but the issue is an important one for it effects both our teaching and evangelism. The first question must therefore be: what role does religious experience play in the Christian life in relation to all its other components? Perhaps most crucially one has to decide whether one can avoid saying with Tillich and the existentialists that everything has to be experienced, so that experience is not only the key factor in religion but in every other discipline.⁷⁰ But this of course leaves unanswered the question of the relative places of religious experience as it is experienced and revelation or other factors as they are experienced.

Perhaps more puzzling is the question as to why there is religious experience in the Christian life at all. Thornton's book is an attempt to answer this question in the face of Jesus' observation that those who have not seen but believed are blessed.⁷¹ In distinguishing between the experience of the Risen Christ to the first disciples and to the present disciples he quotes William Barclay: 'The first appearances of Jesus to his own were evidential... Ever since, the appearances of the risen and ever living Christ have been *sustaining, strengthening* and *renewing*; but the Christ who appears is the same.'⁷² He therefore concludes that religious experience is given to the Church to sustain, strengthen and renew it. It is not something upon which to rely, as one might upon revelation, but it is something to be expected.

Thornton offers one exception when we may rely upon experience. He identifies the sacraments as offering the

69. *Ibid.*, p. 163.
70. P. Tillich, *Systematic Theology* I, London, 1960, pp. 46-52.
71. John 20:29.
72. William Barclay, *Crucified and Crowned*, London, 1961, p. 164 (cited M. Thornton, *My God*, p. 34).

EXPERIENCE IN CHRISTIAN THEOLOGY SINCE BARTH

presence of God in a way which is certain because it depends on his promise. Thus God is experienced by faith on these occasions, even if not by feeling, intuition or the like.[73] Others might wish to include in this category prayer and Bible reading. But the enigmatic nature of religious experience has caught up with us again. Does it make sense to say we can be sure we experience God's presence at the Eucharist or in baptism when we have to admit that we may not feel it in the way we do on other occasions? Thus we are left with the question of whether we are right to expect religious experience on any specific occasions. Mouroux argues that it is not the experience of God which we should desire, but God himself.[74] Perhaps one must conclude that God himself is available to us on certain occasions even when he is not experienced.

Expectation might be thought to lead to wish-fulfilment or self-induced experiences. But Lewis observes that 'undefiled religion puts a premium on integrity and love of truth'[75] which means that the individual has 'to play the game'[76] and yet 'there is no possibility of doubt... when God *does* offer such an experience...'.[77] It is self-authenticating and recognised *a priori*.[78] Nevertheless Mouroux warns 'It is in the region of the senses that the Devil, the Father of lies, is most at home...'.[79] Consequently, we may need to think carefully about how we discern the activity of God; perhaps admitting the possibility of mistakes, whilst affirming with Thornton that the risk is always worth taking: the fear of mistaking the experience for God is no reason for shunning religious experience.[80]

---

73. M. Thornton, *My God*, p. 48; *cf.* J. Mouroux, *The Christian Experience*, p. 191.
74. J. Mouroux, *The Christian Experience*, p. 284.
75. H. D. Lewis, *Our Experience of God*, p. 134f.
76. M. Thornton, *My God*, p. 88.
77. *Ibid.*, p. 90.
78. *Cf.* R. Otto, *The Idea of the Holy* , London, 1959).
79. J. Mouroux, *The Christian Experience*, p. 293.
80. M. Thornton, *My God*, p. 93ff.

Lewis suggests that religious experience characteristically begins in wonder[81] and it issues in worship, understanding and new patterns of life. He concludes that 'the note of stillness rather than violence is that most likely to govern the first dawning of religion and its main moments at all times'[82] although he observes that there is an 'emotional aftersurge'[83] to religious experience 'which energises various other propensities of our nature and sets in train various activities.'[84] He thus agrees with Thornton that religious experiences sustain, strengthen and renew; recognising that they may be of far-reaching effect: 'Religious experiences, like other experiences which have a very distinctive character, are woven into the web of our life as a whole and count for us quite as much in this way very often as they do in themselves.'[85] Indeed, Mouroux suggests that one of the tests of such experiences is whether they issue in right attitudes to God; acts of theological and moral virtue, and mortification or abnegation of the 'old man'.[86]

Mouroux suggests that there are further tests of religious experience.[87] Firstly, it is experiential, understood in personal totality and never merely empirical or experimental. Secondly it is integrating for the individual's own self-understanding and enables integration with the whole of reality as understood. Thirdly, it is voluntary; it is not a state to be endured, but something to which the individual assents: indeed he identifies the rhythm of religious experience as awareness and accepting. Fourthly, it is affective; 'grace gives man a new appetite and new inclinations'.[88] Fifthly, it is active, it leads to total commitment

---

81. H. D. Lewis, *Our Experience of God*, p. 120.
82. *Ibid.*, p. 132.
83. *Ibid.*, p. 137.
84. *Ibid.*, p. 136.
85. *Ibid.*, p. 146.
86. J. Mouroux, *The Christian Experience*, p. 297.
87. *Ibid.*, p. 15.
88. *Ibid.*, p. 270.

for all time, and finally it is social because the God who is experienced is Father of all. Hence, a relationship with him touching everything in a person, is 'a profoundly individual affair, but it can never be individualistic'.[89] Lewis offers a systematic statement of the components of the Christian life.[90] Religious experience he suggests gives rise to perceived patterns of significance. The third order activity is the production of imaginative representations 'images must thus be anchored in experience and never allowed to take wing very far on their own'.[91] Dogmatic reflections on the first three ingredients take us beyond the Christian life into theology proper, and that in turn gives rise to religious symbols; performative activities; sacred places and things.

The Role of Religious Experience in Christian Theology

Lewis has pointed us to the role of religious experience in theology. There is an obvious distinction to be made here. Except in the case of a non-believing theologian, (or even in his case according to Rahner, et. al.) all theologians are susceptible to religious experience throughout their lives and this must have an effect on their work as a whole. This 'hidden' factor is harder to investigate than the explicit use of experience made in theology. But this second category needs a word of explanation. Some theologians claim to be (or not to be) prepared to take religious experience into account, but it is necessary to examine their work to assess how far this is the case.

Technically any area of theology might be influenced by religious experience : we have already made reference to the possibility of religious experience accompanying the sacraments; so we might certainly say that they are to be interpreted religiously. The doctrine of God may be influ-

---

89. *Ibid.*, p. 8.
90. H. D. Lewis, *Our Experience of God*, p. 154ff.
91. *Ibid.*, p. 164.

enced by our experience of him; the doctrine of the Holy Spirit by his influence on us; ecclesiology by our experience of the church local and universal. Examples abound. But because from the beginning the church has claimed that it is possible to meet with the Risen Christ, it is to christology that I turn.

We begin with an examination of a radical article by John Coventry in which he argues that the theological conclusions of *The Myth of God Incarnate* are the inevitable consequences of their methodological starting point.[92] He disagrees with their presuppositions that encounter with Christ through Scripture is the basis of faith; and he does not think that the historical Jesus is the object of faith. He summarises his position thus: 'The historical fact that there never was a Christian faith simply in the mortal Jesus, but only in the risen Christ, seems to me to impose a theological imperative. Whatever we may think our faith rests on, and however we may think it works, the resurrection is a constitutive part of its object and is not to be regarded as part of the apparatus of human interpretation of that object defined as the historical Jesus.'[93] Thus, the belief in the divinity of Christ arose historically 'from belief in the risen Christ, and systematically can only do so.'[94] Both early church and present Christian faith are 'based on encounter with the risen Lord; it is an experience of being encountered or addressed by him; it is a recognition that in this risen Lord, God himself addresses us. We today are able to believe because we are encountered and addressed by the living Lord where he in fact is, dwelling by his Spirit in his Body the Church, and are enabled by the same Spirit to recognise him for who he is. It is primarily in people that we encounter Christ and not in texts: people are the locus of revelation. We do not start from scratch. We enter into

92. J. Coventry, 'The Myth and the Method' *Theology* 81 (1978), pp. 252-261. This article discusses John Hicks (ed.), *The Myth of God Incarnate*, London, 1977.
93. J. Coventry, 'The Myth and the Method', p. 253.
94. *Ibid.*, p. 255.

a living tradition – that is, a shared experience and a shared interpretation of it.'[95] He considers that that encounter or experience can be deepened through reading the Scriptures: 'we encounter Christ in the New Testament, but only because we have first encountered him in people.'[96] Thus he argues that christology must begin with the experience of the Risen Christ.

However, when we turn to contemporary theologians to discover how far they allow their experience of the Risen Christ to inform their theology, we find that there is little evidence of it so doing. The material is summarised conveniently in R. Bauckham's *Knowing God Incarnate*.[97] He suggests that such consideration may be found in D. Bonhoeffer's *Christology*, F. J. van Beeck's *Christ Proclaimed; Christology as Rhetoric*, and P. Schoonenberg's *The Christ*.[98] He also notes that not all theologians are prepared to admit this as part of their data. W. Herrmann presents the nineteenth-century German Liberal Protestant 'rejection of any kind of communion with the exalted Christ',[99] but this position has been argued more recently by G. W. H. Lampe and A. T. Hanson.[100] Bauckham makes the same point as J. Coventry, that experience of Christ may come through the corporate Body of Christ – namely his church,[101] and Mouroux makes much of this point.[102] Once again there are two questions: Is

---

95. *Ibid.*, p. 259.
96. *Ibid.*, p. 260.
97. R. Bauckham, *Knowing God Incarnate*, Grove Spirituality Series (6), Nottingham, 1983.
98. D. Bonhoeffer, *Christology* , London, 1966); F. J. van Beeck, *Christ Proclaimed: Christology as Rhetoric*, New York, 1979; P. Schoonenberg, *The Christ*, London, 1972. (Cited by R. Bauckham, *Knowing God Incarnate*, p. 24).
99. *Ibid.*, p. 24.
100. G. W. H. Lampe, *God as Spirit*, Oxford, 1977; A. T. Hanson, *Image of the Invisible God* , London, 1982). (Cited by R. Bauckham, *Knowing God Incarnate*, p. 5).
101. R. Bauckham, *Knowing God Incarnate*, p. 8.
102. J. Mouroux, *The Christian Experience*, Chap. 7, pp. 18ff.

experience of the Risen Christ still a possibility, or does the evidence not require us to assert more than that we have encountered the Spirit? Having settled that point there is still the question: What part should the experience play in dogmatic theology? Is it the starting point which Coventry asserts, or has it some lesser place? Perhaps most difficult of all would be the question of whether such experience could ever be normative for theology. R. T. France considers that the worship of Jesus was part of the church's experience from the earliest times, and that this has been 'a neglected factor in Christological debate'.[103] Having outlined some New Testament substantiation of this assertion, he concludes 'the attitude of worship towards Jesus is often directly traceable to the Christian's experience of his saving work.'[104] He continues: 'I am suggesting, then, that incarnational Christology of the New Testament had its roots ... in Christian experience of Jesus, both in his earthly ministry and in his risen power, and that it was the natural translation of this experience into an attitude of worship which provided the seedbed for New Testament Christology. To fail to explore and account for this attitude of worship ... is to discard the real life situation of a warm and experience-centered devotion to Jesus in favour of a process of philosophical speculation which lacks an adequate starting point in the life of the Christian church.'[105] C. F. D. Moule argues a similar case in an article offering a threefold thesis: that 'distinctively Christian experience – experience, I repeat, that is recognizable and distinctively Christian – always involves an understanding of Jesus Christ as present.': that there is always an identification of the present risen Christ with

---

103. R. T. France, 'The Worship of Jesus: A Neglected Factor in Christological Debate', in H. H. Rowdon (ed.), *Christ the Lord*, Leicester, 1982.
104. *Ibid.*, p. 33.
105. *Ibid.*, p. 33.

Jesus of Nazareth; and that it is difficult to dismiss these claims because they possess a certain resilience.[106] After a glance at the New Testament he notes that in sacrament, in worship, in hymnology *etc.* this experience is central. But, he observes, this experience is so closely allied to the experience of God himself, that they are not always distinguishable. 'Certainly, I cannot myself claim to have had any direct experience of the living Christ *that could be described as wholly distinct from an experience of God.*'[107] Like Thornton, he affirms that this is part of the normal Christian life,[108] and which therefore cannot be ignored by theology.[109]

Moule's personal comment highlights the problem of description of the Christian experience. Theologically speaking there should be close identification between Jesus and his Father, but not identity. While some have argued that Trinitarian doctrine arose out of the experience of the early Christians,[110] M. Wiles suggests that nothing could be further from the truth.[111] Despite this argument, J. Moltmann has suggested that experience could form the new starting point for his doctrine of the trinity.[112] The role of experience in christology, trinitarian formulations or other doctrines is complicated by the presence of other disputed areas, such as the role of Scripture, philosophy, tradition, and history. The method and content of theology is a confused area, but certainly one where it seems that

106. C. D. F. Moule, 'The Christ of Experience and the Christ of History' *Theology* 81, 1978, p. 164.
107. *Ibid.*, p. 168.
108. *Ibid.*, p. 169f.
109. *Ibid.*, p. 172.
110. *E.g.*, K. E. Kirk, *The Vision of God*, London, 1931.
111. M. Wiles, 'Reflections on the Origins of the Doctrine of the Trinity' in *Working Papers in Doctrine*, London, 1976, p. 11. The ante-Nicene fathers came to accept a trinitarian doctrine 'even though they often found it difficult to interpret their experience of God in this particular threefold way.'
112. J. Moltmann, *The Trinity and the Kingdom of God*, London, 1981, p. 4.

there will continue to be debate about the influence of religious experience.

It would be wrong to conclude without mentioning the way in which experience influences theologians without their conscious consent. David Kelsey in a fascinating volume investigates the way that experience influences the theologian's interpretation and selection of Scripture.[113] Whatever detailed comments one might wish to make on his thesis, it undoubtedly offers genuine insights into the methods of theologians. It is certainly true that in the field of hermeneutics, long before the theologian has education enough to theorise about how to use Scripture, he has years of Christian experience in worship and private devotions which may be very influential on his life. Indeed, if we remember that religious experience may be experience understood religiously, we may recognise that in the life experiences of those who have pioneered liberation or feminist theology, there has been much to influence the way that they handle Scripture, and perhaps what are the key issues in theology today. Perhaps one example may suffice in an area which must be speculative. Reading J. Moltmann's *Experiences of God* one cannot but be struck by his description of the prisoner of war experience.[114] 'I saw how other men collapsed inwardly, how they gave up all hope, sickening for the lack of it, some of them dying. The same thing almost happened to me. What kept me from it was a rebirth to new life thanks to a hope for which there was no evidence at all.

'It was not that I experienced any sudden conversion .... It was nothing very overwhelming. And yet the experience of misery and forsakenness and daily humiliation gradually built up into an experience of God.'[115] He describes eloquently the experience of being within barbed

---

113. D. Kelsay, *The Uses of Scripture in Recent Theology*, London, 1975.
114. J. Moltmann, *Experiences of God*, London, 1980.
115. *Ibid.*, p. 7ff.

wire fences, and of God 'as the power of hope and pain';[116] concluding: 'I cannot even say I found God there. But I do know in my heart that it is there that he found me, and that I would otherwise have been lost.'[117] Such an experience helps one to see why this person has written a *Theology of Hope*[118] and made eschatology a key feature of so much of his thinking.

The evangelical tradition in which we stand has long considered that that religious experience is part of the normal Christian life. We have seen that Roman Catholicism is prepared to admit that, and other traditions such as Anglo-Catholocism. Under the influence of the existentialist philosophy with which we are surrounded, and with the claims of charismatic Christian brethren sounding in our ears, perhaps this century was bound to take up the discussion whose agenda was set in part by the Schleiermacher-Barth debate, and which has been given fresh impetus by the claim of other faiths equally to experience the divine. This paper has tried to show how some are meeting the challenge, and it is one which despite its complexity, must be resolved. Our traditions and our faith give us special reasons to make a major and unique contribution to the debate.

Conclusion

In making that contribution we might wish to consider the following affirmations.

'Religious experience' may be appropriately claimed in different circumstances. Firstly, all experience can be understood religiously since the Christian believes that nothing occurs outside of the providential care of God, and nothing need occur without his gracious blessing. Indeed, we rightly ask the question 'what does God want me to learn through the events of today?' even when we have no

---

116. *Ibid.*, p. 8ff.
117. *Ibid.*, p. 9.
118. J. Moltmann, *Theology of Hope*, London, 1967.

very clear perception of his activity or presence. Frequently, of course, that question cannot be answered in an immediate way, for we require the passage of time to assess the significance of events. Secondly, in that overall context, there are some 'ordinary' moments of life about which we would wish to say that God was especially present, or that we were especially conscious of his presence. Thirdly, there are 'trysting places' such as prayer, baptism, eucharist, the reading and proclamation of God's word, where God has promised to be present with his people, which, while they should never presume upon the experience of God, neither should they be surprised by its occurrence. Finally, there are some extra-ordinary events, such as visions or miracles through which God makes himself known in a very clear way.

Of all these religious experiences, however, Christians would have to say that the presence and experience of God is never universally demonstrable, never absolutely incontrovertible, never unequivocal. Moreover, there would be two good theological reasons for this, that they would want to offer. The first of these lies within the nature of God himself; the second within the nature of humanity. The transcendent otherness of God, his self-giving love which offers men and women freedom, together produce a situation in which God has never, not even in the Incarnation, given people such an experience as will compel their love and obedience. Such an experience must be that to which we look forward at the end time. This primary reason for the enigmatic nature of religious experience is echoed by a secondary reason within ourselves which springs from our finite frailty. Although we may experience God, our descriptions can never capture him, and our sinfulness renders us liable to misunderstand or even rebel against our encounter.

If this is indeed the case, it is important to maintain the distinction between revelation and religious experience. It may be that this differentiation can only be made by the religious community with hindsight. Much of what we now count as revelation began in individual or corporate experience, both 'secular' and 'religious'. All religious experience has an immediacy about it, which does not require months or years to pass before it is claimed as such. Generally, people claim that category for it on the spot. Further, it is paradoxically the case that although it is inherently enigmatic, it nevertheless carries complete conviction with it for the person who has experienced it. Such conviction however has to be tested by the passage of time: at a distance it may be possible to acknowledge that it was illusion, delusion or the like; immediately that is unlikely to happen.

Consequently not all religious experience can or should be elevated to the realm of revelation. As with historical events, God added his word of interpretation to religious experience either before, concurrently, or after, and the community weighed the word, judged the prophet, tested the spirits, and finally recognised that in the event and the interpretation *combined* God had revealed himself. This should not be considered as the community deciding what is to be considered as revelation, although they have their part to play. Although the community needs to recognise God's revelation, only God can give the combination of events, fulfilment of prophecy, inherent rightness of interpretation which together give rise to such recognition. Even exceptional religious experiences such as miracles need to be assessed as to their source and their meaning.

However religious experience as distinct from revelation has to be considered as part of the data of dogmatic theology. It rightly can query the balance and emphases of theology. The church has an important role to play when it says to the dogmatic theologian 'But we don't experience it that way!' And the theologian has an important role to play when he addresses the church and says that 'This is the truth of God: what is keeping you from experiencing his grace and forgiveness?' for example. There is an essential dialogue here.

This is possible because the experience of the church and the doctrine of the theologian are both themselves to be in dialogue with the same revelation of God. Our experience of God is checked by and interpreted in the light of the revelation of God in Christ Jesus and in the scriptures. If it is genuinely experience of the God who is already known in Christ, it can be regarded as true, although it may not be regarded as 'the truth' since our explanation of it may be influenced more by our context than by God's perspective. For this reason while it may influence our theology it should not be normative.

The religious experiences of mankind outside the Christian community cannot be regarded as experiences of God the Father of our Lord Jesus Christ without a great deal of difficulty. It is difficult to think that God is content that thousands should experience him, but misunderstand him and that to their secret salvation. It is at least arguable that this is more problematic than the more traditional view that they do not know him at all. Secondly, those who would give positive assessment to the experience of those outside of Christianity need to explain how they account for the biblical material including references to masquerade of Satan as an angel of light: the possibility of experiences occurring which are falsely thought to originate with God.

Although religious experience is prone to misuse or abuse, nevertheless it has been part of the evangelical tradition, focusing around conversion, but not exclusively there. There remains a real need for this to be developed and explored so that we can make our contribution to the church as a whole.

THE EXPERIENCE OF CONVERSION

HELMUT BURKHARDT

If the question of the experience of conversion is posed in the context of the overall theme of 'Christian experience', this broader perspective makes it clear that our concern is not simply with experience but with Christian experience, and this, I believe, should first and foremost always be experience of God. With this limitation of our theme, therefore, purely secular experiences of conversion in the sense of a general moral, ideological or other religious reorientation are excluded. Our question would therefore be more closely defined in this sense: to what extent is an experience of God involved in Christian conversion?

In the tradition of theology there are very many different answers to the question how God can be experienced in general and in particular through conversion.

At the one extreme there is the so-called (Erlangen) theology of experience, which explains Christian experience as the absolute basis of theology as follows: 'I, the Christian, am my own subject of knowledge to myself as theologian.'[1] Here one begins specifically with the experience of being born again, but not only in such a way that, corresponding to an old requirement of evangelical piety, the state of being born again is required of the theologian as a prerequisite, that being born again is so to speak, the door of entrance to theology, but also in such a way that the experience of being born again is at the same time the source which provides theology with its substance.

Behind this conception there lies in the history of ideas I. Kant's critique of knowledge; he had called all knowledge of God into question and separated faith from it. In this way, however, God had been banished from earthly reality as far as knowledge of him was concerned.

---

1. J. Chr. Hofmann, *Der Schriftbeweis*, 1857, pp. 1, 10.

With the stimulation and encouragement afforded by Schleiermacher's recourse to the simple feeling of dependence as the religious *a priori,* the Erlangen theology of experience thought that room for God could again be found in our reality, that in Christian experience this Archimedian point could be seen, securely set against all philosophical scepticism.[2]

The other extreme is found as a conscious antithesis specifically (but not exclusively) to the Erlangen theology in the so-called dialectic theology. At least for the followers of Karl Barth this amounted virtually to an outlawing of experience. Barth himself was more cautious here. For he conceded absolutely the possibility of Christian experience in a certain way. He even argued polemically against 'the complementary pessimistic form of self-assertion in which we will have nothing to do with events of which the content is the gift and appropriation of faith. We defiantly dispute the reality of such things. We scornfully interpret whatever we hear from others in this respect as illusion and ecstatic fantasy. We contentedly accept the fact that in our own lives such things never have been and never will be.'[3]

Barth can even admit: 'It is not to be denied . . . that in certain humanly identifiable moments and situations, not simply in recollection or expectation but in the concrete present of faith, we are in fact humbly and thankfully aware in a very special way, not merely of our state of believing, but of our real faith, and therefore of our whole life as a life lived in God, and that in this sense we gladly recall such moments as certainly significant.'[4] But scarcely have these words flowed off the tip of his pen before he states again the fundamental ambiguity of all such experience and de-

2. See the critical analysis of the Erlangen theology of experience in M. Kähler, *Geschichte der protestantischen Dogmatik im 19.Jht.,* pp. 212-235, and E. Schaeder, *Theozentrische Theologie,* pp. 1, 3-50.
3. CD 1:2, p. 707.
4. *Ibid.,* p. 708.

THE EXPERIENCE OF CONVERSION

clares as his own proposition: 'The really outstanding events of our life, upon which our faith lives and in which our whole life is revealed to us in faith as life in God, ... are simply identical with our share in the great acts of God in His revelation.'[5] Again: 'those individual and definite events in which, according to the Bible, God's self-revelation is fulfilled, ... constitute the reality of the faith-events of our own life.'[6] Thereby Barth swings over into the existential Platonism which is typical of him and in which history loses its own reality. Barth then makes his meaning clear in an anecdote about Kohlbrügge, who, when asked the date of his conversion, is supposed to have said: 'At Golgotha', an answer which Barth agrees with, even if he makes a distinction between the virtual (then) and the actual (now, in faith). Yet despite this distinction this trend of thought tends without doubt in the direction of a non-realization of God acting in the present, which is roughly expressed in the rhetorical question: 'Is there a miracle story that I can relate from my own life, which ... will not be totally dissolved in this divine miracle story [sc. from the past], and which therefore will hardly be worth relating [separately and] *in abstracto*?'[7]

In the different answers given to the question of Christian experience at both of these extremes we find some basic viewpoints expressed: in the theology of experience we can see a – justified – intention to push forward through theological knowledge to reality, to 'the things themselves', over against all scepticism or even mere spectulation. 'To know as one travels [towards the

---

5. *Ibid.*, p. 708.
6. *Ibid.*
7. *Ibid.*, p. 709. The question whether Barth came later to a more positive evaluation of experience can be left out of consideration, since this essay is orientated not towards the history of theology but towards systematic theology, and the thought of Barth in the first volumes of the Church Dogmatics was introduced only as an example of one possible fundamental systematic position.

things]' – this is indeed etymologically the original sense of the verb 'to experience'. In view of this no reference to a formal authority is needed, *i.e.* to an authority that has come down to us from the past (an old concern of Enlightenment criticism); at the same time by starting from experience we avoid mere inherited counterfiet piety (an old concern of Pietism).

In the case of dialectic theology there comes into effect an – equally justified – resistance against the anthropocentrism, to which the theology of experience all too easily succumbs; resistance against the danger that faith perhaps rests upon highly subjective experiences of one's psyche (and falls with them); finally – and almost more dangerous – that faith in a person searching for available 'experiences' eventually turns in upon itself and indeed – what in no way makes the matter but rather worse – upon its religious self, the self which enjoys its own religiousity.

The question to what extent we can indeed speak, or not speak at all, of real experience *of God*, and furthermore, in view of our specific theme, in connection with conversion, is to be considered in what follows on the basis of an analysis of appropriate biblical material.

What is Conversion?

Even outside the Christian faith there is certainly a type of experience to be found that we may be inclined to describe as one of conversion: the experience of a fundamental, more or less sudden change with regard to one's morality and world view.[8] Occasionally even in ancient writings we

---

8. *Cf.*, for example the definition given by A. D. Nock, *Conversion*, p. 7: 'the reorientation of the soul of an individual, his deliberate turning from indifference, or from an earlier form of piety to another, a turning which implies consciousness that a great change is involved, that the old was wrong and the new is right.' *Cf.* W. James, *The Varieties of Religious Experience*: conversion signifies 'the gradual or sudden process..., through which a split self, aware of its perversity, reaches inner unity,

find a terminology that comes close to the biblical form of expression.[9] And yet at no point, either then or today, does the idea of conversion play a central role that comes anywhere near what it does in the biblical tradition. This fact can ultimately be understood only in the light of the uniqueness of the knowledge of God in the Bible: the God of the Bible is not one of many powers to be honoured according to their kind and as they can be used,[10] but he is the Sovereign Creator of the world and Lord of history, who has a claim on the whole life of a person. His election of Israel to be his people and a blessing for all peoples (Gn. 12:2f; Ex. 19:5f.) is the presupposition for the biblical idea of conversion: the prophetic call to conversion (Heb. *shub*) is a call to *re*turn to an obedience to God that corresponds to his elective choice, an obedience that summons the whole man to love his God 'with all his heart, with all his soul, and with all his strength' (Dt. 6:5). Evidence for this call to repentance is found, for example, in the historical books (*e.g.* 1 Sa. 7:3; 2 Ki. 17:13) and in the majority of the writing prophets (especially Amos, Hosea, Isaiah, Jeremiah and Ezekiel).

This call to repentance is then taken up in the NT, but under changed salvation-historical conditions. Negatively, the history of Israel attested to us in the OT had proved that Israel was not really ready and ultimately was not able to undergo the turning back with their hearts that was demanded by God (Je. 13:23; *cf.* Mt. 19:26).[11] Positively, the call to turn back went out once again through Jesus and his disciples, but now with a new positive presupposition, namely that of the presence of the Kingdom of God in

---

so that from this time on it knows itself to be on the right road and feels uplifted and happy.'
9. *Cf.* O. Michel, 'Die Umkehr in der Verkündigung Jesu', Ev. Theol. 1938, pp. 403f.
10. *Cf.* A. D. Nock, *op. cit.*, p. 14: 'A man used Mithraism, but he did not belong to it body and soul.'
11. See the literature cited by H. Burkhardt, *Die biblische Lehre von der Bekehrung*, pp. 12-15, 21.

Jesus as an offer of God's grace on the basis of Jesus' suffering and dying for the sins not only of Israel but of the whole world (Mt. 20:28; Jn. 1:21). On account of the universal significance of Jesus the offer of repentance is now open to all: not only – in the case of Israel – as a call to return to the Abraham/Sinai covenant, but now also – in the case of the heathen – as a call to return to the status *post lapsum* of man made in the image of God. In this way, to be sure, the NT reality explodes the old pictures: the redemption offered in Jesus is more than the mere restoration of the fomer kind. To be a child of God is more than being made in God's image.

As far as our theme is concerned, this short statement of what is understood by 'conversion' in the Bible makes it clear that conversion is at any time an event embedded in the history of God with his people, that it is based afresh on the event of God speaking and acting in this history – and to this extent it takes place in the area of what can be experienced. What this experience depends on, of course, is not so much people being able to go through this or that enriching experience, but on people responding to the spoken word of God in obedience through faith.

How Does Conversion Take Place?

After this outline of what conversion is in the Bible, the question of how it takes place should lead us to a more exact understanding of the relationship between conversion and experience.

Since the Gospels are without doubt of lasting, fundamental importance for the NT message, we begin with an analysis of their testimony, and specifically with the synoptic Gospels, since John's Gospel does not use the concept of conversion (for John see below).

The synoptic Gospels for their part begin not with Jesus' call to repentance but with John the Baptist's. Matthew presents it in a form of words which is identical with that of Jesus' call to repentance (Mt. 4:17): 'Repent for the kindom of heaven is at hand' (Mt. 3:2).

THE EXPERIENCE OF CONVERSION

The first part of this summary contains a summons to act. This summons is illustrated by v. 6, 'and they confessed their sins and were baptised', and is continued in v. 8, 'produce fruit befitting repentance' (*cf.* also what Jesus says in Mt. 7:16-20), and indeed, as v. 10 says, 'good' fruit. Matthew gives only this picture, while Luke in the so-called 'ethical teaching' of the Baptist gives it a more concrete content. According to Luke repentance has to do with a new, just (i.e. appropriate to society) way of living (Lk. 3:10-14).

The second part of the summary contains a declaration of a future act of God which is the basis of the summons in the first part: a declaration of the approaching Kingdom of God. The context elucidates this further. John may be thinking primarily of the execution of judgement in connection with the coming Kingdom of God (*cf.* v. 10, the cutting down of the branches of the tree as a symbol of the rejection of members of the chosen people) as an expression of God's anger (v. 7b). The judgment will be executed by the coming 'Mightier One (v. 11) who will baptise not with water but 'with the Spirit and fire'. 'Fire' here is generally understood as a symbol of the Spirit, and one-sidedly as a gift of salvation. In my view this interpretation is by no means certain. According to the context of John's message (v. 10) and in the light of Is. 4:4, what is to be reckoned with is rather a purifying act of judgment (and to that extent a preparation for salvation).[12]

In Mark too the Baptist's message has two crucial points. John preaches a 'baptism of repentance for the forgiveness of sins' (Mk. 1:4). Here repentance, to which one testifies by being baptised, refers to the fact that people find forgiveness of sins in the judgment of God and thus, as Matthew puts it, they 'escape the future wrath'. (Mt. 3:7b).

---

12. T. Zahn, *Comm. ad loc.*, p. 140, 'a picture of the flaming and devouring anger of God in judgment'.

As already mentioned, Jesus takes up this message of John the Baptist, but characteristically with a different emphasis, as Mark's summary makes particularly clear. Here at the outset the whole message of Jesus is editorially summed up in terms of the gospel (1:14). In the words of Jesus himself it is as follows:

The time is fulfilled,
and the kingdom of God is at hand;
repent
and believe in the gospel. (Mk. 1:15).

The two parts have here each become two pairs of parallel clauses. In view of this the perfect 'is fulfilled' interprets the 'is at hand' in the sense of the present reality of the Kingdom of God; the summons to belief in the good news, however, interprets the call to repentance as an invitation to accept the *gracious* presence of God, *i.e.*, in terms of the language of 1:4, the forgiveness of sins already promised (*cf.* Mk. 2:10).

In Luke these summaries which are placed so emphatically at the beginning of Jesus' activity in Mt. and Mk. are missing. However, to a certain extent in Lk. the so-called inaugural sermon of Jesus in Nazareth corresponds to them. According to this sermon the prophecy in Isaiah is fulfilled in Jesus ('Today it has been fulfilled', Lk. 4:21): someone will come in the power of the Holy Spirit and 'will bring good news to the poor' (Lk. 4:18). The call to repentance is missing at this point in Lk. but is found in 5:32, a formula which similarly describes Jesus' mission in summary form (only the phrase 'to repentance' is missing in the otherwise identical parallels in Mt. and Mk.).

We meet the keyword 'repentance' once again in the Gospels in a similar summary form in the reports of the sending out of the disciples (Mk. 6:12: 'and they went out and preached that people should repent'; *cf.* the post-Easter commission in Lk. 24:47: '. . . that forgiveness of sins should be preached in his name to all nations'; in the sending out of the disciples by Jesus before Easter Lk. 9:2 only has 'to preach the Kingdom of God and to heal', while Matthew says nothing about the content of the message).

We find further mention of repentance, again without a more precise definition, in the words of judgment of Jesus upon those who rejected his call to repentance, namely in the cry of woe over the Galilean towns (Mt. 11:20f. = Lk. 10:13), in the announcement of judgement upon the 'present generation' with whom the repentant people of Nineveh are contrasted (Mt. 12:41 = Lk. 11:32), and also in the word of judgement which follows Pilate's shedding of blood in Galilee and the fall of the tower of Siloam (Lk. 13:5).

A few observations may be made on this material. In Mt. 11:20f, it is the mighty acts of Jesus (acts of healing and casting out demons) which should have prompted repentance, which now make the rejection of the call to repentance a yet heavier burden of guilt. The mighty acts are here understood as signs of the presence of the Kingdom of God; they occur through the powerful commanding word of Jesus (Mt. 12:28). In Mt. 12:41, on the other hand, there is a warning against egoistical misunderstanding and misuse of the signs of Jesus and reference is made to the Word as the source of repentance (the people of Nineveh 'repented at the preaching of Jonah') and to the unique power of the words of Jesus ('something greater than Jonah is here').

In Lk. 13 the negative point of reference in the call to repentance is expounded: the sins of mankind. Here the universality of the verdict is noteworthy ('if you do not repent, you will die') – although no concrete reason is evident. 'All the stories of Jesus' teaching and life show that everyone who meets him without exception stands under the sentence of death and perdition.'[13]

---

13. J. Schniewind, 'Das Gleichnis vom verlorenen Sohn', in: *Die Freude der Busse*, 1960, p. 66.

Finally, alongside these more purely summary statements about conversion we find the event of conversion illustrated in a few of Jesus' parables which Luke transmits to us (Lk. 15 and 16:19-31).
An outstanding feature of the parables of repentance in Lk. 15 is their description of the call to repentance as gospel.[14] That is why it is a cause for joy,[15] and indeed not just for the repentant person himself (*cf.* also Lk. 19:5; Acts 8:39). What Lk. 15 is all about is that it is also for those who share in the experience of repentance (vs. 7, 10; *cf.* v. 32). This joy is, however, scarcely conceivable if all acts of repentance really only happen in the twilight, in which Barth thinks they should be seen.

In Lk. 16 in the parable of 'the rich man and poor Lazarus' what is of interest for our enquiry is that according to v. 31 the conversion of the rich man's brother comes about, if at all, as a result of the Word (in the mouth of Abraham: the law and the prophets), not through wonderful events like a resurrection from the dead. These by themselves could never bring about the inner change of heart through which man surrenders to God's sovereign claim on him and at the same time to his judgment of his sins, and on account of this turns to the one who only can help him out of the perdition which he has thus experienced.

Specially clear examples of how conversion can take place are offered, of course, by reports of conversions such as those of Peter (Lk. 5:1-11) and Zacchaeus (Lk. 19:1-10), and also less directly of the woman who was 'a great sinner' (Lk. 7:36-50).

Peter is terrified (5:9) when he recognises through the miracle the person with whom he has to do. Through this recognition of Jesus comes at the same time the recogni-

---

14. *Cf.* J. Schniewind, *op. cit.*, 60, in a comment on 15:16: 'Repentance is only of a right nature when it springs out of remembrance of God and his goodness'.
15. *Cf.* Schniewind's whole exegesis of Lk. 15, as well as the essay 'Die Freude im NT' in the same volume, pp. 9ff.

THE EXPERIENCE OF CONVERSION

tion of himself as a sinner (v. 8). Forgiveness is implicitly contained in the call and is achieved by Peter's following that call.

That Zacchaeus is a sinner does not need to be spelled out – every one already knows it (19:7). It may be that with Zacchaeus too, and in his wish to see Jesus, the desire to be free from the burden of guilt and the sin causing it is implicitly expressed. The fact that Jesus goes into his home of all homes against expectations is a signal to him that his wish is being fulfilled; Jesus then explicitly confirms this (v. 9f). But even before Jesus says this, Zacchaeus draws the practical consequences out of his being accepted (v. 8). It is in the whole event, however, that repentance takes place.

The story of the sinful woman, which is mentioned only in passing in connection with the report of a conversation at table between Jesus and a Pharisee, does not properly depict the conversion itself but basically presupposes it and speaks of its consequences: the love for Jesus springing out of the reception of forgiveness of sins (7:47f). The tears (tears of joy?) are certainly evidence of a strong inner reaction which includes emotions.

Last, but not necessarily least, the whole so-called ethical preaching of Jesus is to be taken into account in our discussion, above all as it is summarised in Matthew's Sermon on the Mount. For the whole, widely known and puzzling radicalism of its demands can be understood only in the context of Jesus' call to repentance. Only he who follows this call, thereby receiving 'a new existence' (Schniewind) can fulfil them. Conversely the radical earnestness of conversion becomes clear through the very radicalism of these demands.[16]

16. *Cf.* J. Schniewind, 'Was verstand Jesus unter Umkehr?', in *Die Freude der Busse*, p. 25: 'Jesus' whole preaching is a call to repentance'; and A. Schlatter, *Geschichte des Christus*, 1921, p. 174: Jesus' 'ethical pronouncements' were 'not meditations about problems of an ethical nature, but integral parts of his call to repentance.'

Helmut Burkhardt

Conversion and Experience: a Summary and Systematic Evaluation of the Exegetical Analysis

I would like to try and sum up the context in which the Gospels speak of repentance under three aspects:

1. *The background, which indicates the necessity of conversion*, according to the witness of the Gospels, is the recognition of the sins of mankind and the coming judgment upon them. The seriousness of the judgment corresponds to the radicalism (Paul: enmity towards God) and universality (Paul: 'there is no one who is righteous') of sin; the judgment is concerned with eternal rejection or acceptance, death or life; this also explains the radicalism of the call to repentance, which urges not only renunciation of this or that sin but a fundamental rejection of sin.

But who is capable of such repentance? Nobody! (Mt. 19:26). Consequently, there is something else to be said:

2. *The background, which indicates the possibility of conversion*, is the revelation of God in Christ, the presence of the Kingdom of God in his person, already now brought to focus in the authoritative exhortation to receive the forgiveness of sins.

3. Finally: *the horizon which indicates the goal of conversion*, is the sovereign rule of God, whose authority the repentant person now already acknowledges (the request in Mt. 6:10b, 'Your will be done on earth as it is in heaven' explains the preceding request for the Kingdom to come in v. 10a).

Now because in conversion there is genuine deliverance on the basis of genuine redemption in Christ for genuine service for God, such conversion is likewise a genuine event in our personal history as a response to an imperative and hence as an act. As such, however, it is also an experience. As such, be it noted, not primarily as a result

THE EXPERIENCE OF CONVERSION

of the accompanying and scarcely avoidable (why should they be?) emotional elements for living people such as joy (*cf. e.g.* Mt. 13:44; *et al.*) or pain (*cf.* Lk. 15:126; *et al.*). As an event in space and time, therefore, conversion is in actual fact an experience, and moreover not simply experience of a worldly nature or confined to oneself, but a real experience of *God* which takes place in the personal certainty of the righteousness and holiness of the biblical command, of the condemnation of our sin, and of the impenetrable reality of the forgiveness promised in the gospel.[17]

On the other hand, we must beware lest the knowledge of conversion as an experience may possibly lead to fatal misunderstandings and false conclusions.

First of all, we must remain aware of the fact that the word 'experience' in its everyday usage does have a certain affinity to the emotional. This is true also of conversion as an experience to the extent that it also is generally interwoven with emotional strands. In the case of such a decisive event as conversion, which divides one's whole life into a before and after, this is not all that surprising. And yet the view that the emotional aspect in no way constitutes the essence of the act of conversion must be adhered to. Conversion entails neither simply feeling and emotion (in the sense more or less of *metamelomai*), nor just a change of mind (*metanoia* in its original Greek sense).[18] It is much more than that: essentially it is an act of the whole person, proceeding from the core of his being; biblically speaking it is repentance of the heart, conscious, deliberate subordination of the whole person under God's will (in the sense of the OT *shub*).

---

17. 'We have our righteousness in the midst of the constant experience of our sinfulness', A. Schlatter, *Das christliche Dogma*, 1911, p. 483; *cf.* H. Cremer, *Die christliche Lehre von den Eigenschaften Gottes*, 1897, 1984³, p. 24: The love of God towards the sinner 'is the highest voluntary act that can be conceived.'
18. O. Michel, *Die Umkehr*, p. 403.

What must also be understood is that conversion is not only an inner process but basically a correlative event; it is not just a transformation of the person in himself but is always a turning to God and therefore always takes place in relation to the objective reality of God in his revelation. What the self 'experiences' in conversion is only one aspect of this event and by no means the most important.

Let us clarify this with an example. At the beginning of his Gospel Matthew sums up the meaning of Jesus' mission with an explanation of his name: 'He will save his people from their sins.' Let us just imagine for a moment that someone wished to translate freely: 'Jesus came to procure for us the experience of salvation'; this would make it clear how through the emphasis on the aspect of experience a truly problematic subjectifying of the utterance would result.

Nevertheless, in our time, when theology in general tends far too much simply to sublimate the real nature not only of conversion but also of God and to leave the nature of our reality to secularism, there may well be some good in for once speaking with some emphasis (though not without the appropriate caution) of *experience* of God in a general sense and specifically with regard to conversion.

The Relationship of the Concept of Conversion to Other Soteriological Concepts in the Bible

Up till now, in the presentation of the NT records of conversion, we have confined ourselves to the Synoptic Gospels. This is not quite proper insofar as the post-Easter community undoubtedly took up the message of conversion entrusted to it by Jesus (Lk. 24:47) and mirrored this in the other NT writings, in particular in Acts, occasionally in Paul (even in a so-called 'classical' abbreviated form of the content of the original Christian missionary preaching, 1 Th. 1:9f.), but also in 1 Peter and in the Letter to the Hebrews. In the process, in Acts and in 1 Peter the Greek term *metanoia* recedes before the translation, usually found in the LXX, of the Hebrew *shub* by *epistrepho*.

But our restriction so far to the synoptic Gospels is not ultimately completely irresponsible, since the occurrence of the concept in the NT is actually concentrated on them, while the other witnesses in the NT have in part expressed the same content by means of other concepts.

1. *Conversion and New Birth*

The concept of new birth in the Johanine writings is a particularly good example of how in another tradition a different concept can simply take the place of the concept of 'conversion'. The concept of conversion as a sign of beginning the Christian life is not found at all in John's Gospel or the Letters of John. Only the Revelation of John has it in two places (9:20f.; 16:9,11). Instead John is familiar with the terminology of new birth, which on the other hand is completely absent from the Synoptics, at least in this sense. The term 'new birth' also signifies the beginning of the Christian life.[19] New birth too is an entry into a new existence which stands in opposition to that determined by the sin/the 'flesh'. Whoever is not born again cannot see the Kingdom of God (Jn. 3:3). In this word picture there is expressed particularly powerfully the fact that the step from the old into the new existence is not possible through human energy but only through the working of God's Holy Spirit in man. (3:5-8; *cf*.1:12).

However, this does not happen in a sort of mystical or similarly undefinable way. Rather, this working of the Spirit is founded upon the redeeming work of Jesus (3:14-18; *cf*. Tit. 3:4), mediated by the authoritative spoken word of the Spirit (Jn. 3:34; *cf*. 15:3; 20:22f., as well as 1 Pet. 1:3, 23). As such it works in man the 'renewal' (*anakainosis*, Tit. 3:5), which expresses itself in a changed way of life (Tit. 3:3; *cf*. 2:11f.). So conversion and new birth both sig-

---

19. See H. Burkhardt, *The Biblical Doctrine of Regeneration*, 1978, pp. 19, 23-25.

nify the same event, that of becoming a Christian, only with different theological emphases. A possible historical bridge between the two traditions might be seen on the one hand in Mt. 18:3 and on the other hand in Jn. 3:3.

If, however, we separate new birth and conversion from one another as two different experiences, we fall into the danger of falsifying both concepts. If we place conversion prior to new birth as the human preparation for the latter, we end up in synergism; if we allow new birth as a divine activity to precede conversion as a merely human activity, we end up in mysticism or sacramentalism.

2. *Conversion and faith*

Especially in Paul, as is well known, the concept of faith moves into the centre of his soteriological assertions. But already in the Synoptic witness the concepts of faith and conversion are placed together (Mk. 1:15). Faith is here the act, implied in conversion, of entrusting oneself to God on the basis of the gospel. In John the concept of faith can stand side by side with the concrete picture of new birth (Jn. 3:16). Above all, in Acts (3:19 and elsewhere) and also in Paul (Rom. 13:11; Gal. 2:16) the beginning of the Christian life is marked by the aorist of *pisteuo* ('come to faith').

On the other hand, much more than this is contained in the concept of faith, and therefore it is not as suitable for use as a *terminus technicus* as the concept of conversion is. As a believer one's belief must prove itself in the ever-new act of faith (Acts 16:15; *cf.* Gal. 2:16b; correspondingly conversion can indeed be spoken of in practical terms in the sense of repeated penitence, as, for example, in Rev. 2-3, but, on the whole, the concept of conversion has now developed into the *terminus technicus* for the beginning of the Christian life).

3. *Conversion and Justification*

Yet more emphatic than the concept of faith is that of justification, which denotes the prominent form of apostolic teaching in Paul for us. In Paul justification is, so to speak, the more strongly objective concept which is complementary to the more subjective one of faith. Justification is the gracious justifying sentence of God at the last judgment (*cf.* Rom. 2:13,16). Paul can speak again and again of this judgment as justification in its future form (Gal. 2:16 = Rom. 3:20; Rom. 3:30; *cf.* 5:19; 8:24). Where, on the other hand, he uses the past form, he is evidently thinking of justification as a present promise of the future final verdict (Rom. 5:1, 9; 8:30; Cor. 6:11; Tit. 3:7).

Thus the state of being justified is a characterising mark of the Christian's state of being a Christian. Hence, as may be seen to be presupposed in all the places just mentioned, in Rom. 3:25 justification can expressly describe the transition from the pre-Christian to the Christian position. Corresponding to this is the fact that in Tit. 3 Paul interprets the word picture of new birth (v. 5) in terms of justification.

We must also take note of the fact that according to Paul justification implies the forgiveness of sins (Rom. 4:7). However, as we have seen, the same is true also of the process of conversion from the beginning. Thus justification, like new birth and conversion, stands at the beginning of the Christian life. In contrast with these, however, it not only stands at the beginning, but must constantly be claimed anew in faith, as long as we are in fresh need of forgiveness, that is, as long as we live. Thus faith here stands in antithesis to the experience of one's own sins and bases its certainty of salvation not first and foremost on experience (which is at first only experience of the opposite of salvation), but on the word of forgiveness imparted to the believer. Conversion, understood as implying justification, is thus the beginning of justification which encompasses the whole life of the Christian.

4. *Conversion and Sanctification*
In defining the relationship between conversion and sanctification the starting point is the designation of the

Christian as a 'saint' (1 Cor. 1; 2; and elsewhere). According to this sanctification is not something that is realised at some point of time in the Christian's life, but it is first and foremost something that is there from the beginning of the Christian life. Sanctification can be paraphrased as being enlisted for service for God. It is exactly this after all, as we have seen, that takes place at conversion also.

Rom. 6:17-19 describes the fundamental turn-about in the act of becoming a Christian: Before you became Christians, you were slaves of sin, but now, as Christians, you have become obedient from the heart to the teaching to which you were committed (v. 19); from that there now follows: yield your members to the service of righteousness so that they become sanctified (v. 19; *cf.* v. 22). Here it becomes clear that that which in principle is given in the act of becoming a Christian is at the same time a goal which we are to strive for throughout life.

Here also it is true to say that, just as in the case of justification, conversion is the beginning of sanctification, which encompasses the whole life of the Christian.

5. *Conversion and Baptism of the Spirit or 'Second Blessing'*

First and foremost, it is important to hold fast to the fact that becoming a Christian is always a work of the Holy Spirit (through the Word), as is particularly clear in the biblical testimony about the new birth, but is also expressed in the dependence of conversion on the word of the gospel.

Acts 2:38 'Repent and be baptised, every one of you, for the forgiveness of sins, and you will receive the gift of the Holy Spirit.' The gift of the Spirit is here clearly placed at the beginning of the Christian life. The separating in time of repentance, baptism, and the receiving of the Spirit merely corresponds to the graphic narrative style. This is confirmed above all in Paul's preaching: 'Did you receive the Spirit by works of the law or by the (first, evangelistic) preaching of the faith? ... in the Spirit you have begun ...' (Gal. 3:2f.). But Paul is even more unambiguously clear in Rom. 8: 'Anyone who does not have the Spirit of Christ is not his (and therefore is not a Christian, v. 9b; *cf.* vs. 14-16, 23f.).

And yet the gift of the Spirit is not simply an event of the past. The presence of the Spirit may not be objectively conceived of. It is the personal presence of God as an operative presence.

However, this presence must not be sought after only as a 'second experience' at some point, but ever anew we need the powerful presence of the Spirit in order to be able to live as Christians (*cf.* Eph. 3;16ff.; Ph. 1:9-11; *cf.* Gal. 5;22).

Conversion and Theology – Or, Must One be Converted to be a Theologian?

It must be said first and foremost that in principle in the Bible the activity of the mind is not an activity independent of the other vital functions of the numan being (*cf.* Pr. 1:7).

Further, the mind is thus also included in the human condition of fallenness in sin (Eph. 4:18; Rom. 1; 21f; 1 Cor. 2; 214; *cf.* Is. 29:9ff.). This fundamental realisation should not, however, make us jump to the conclusion that the foolishness of the unbeliever (1 Cor. 1; 20) is simply to be equated with stupidity and narrow-mindedness. Rather, there is here an analogy between thinking and willing. In Rom. 7:18 Paul says: I can have the desire all right, but not the ability to fulfil it, and this moreover with regard to the radically understood obedience to God's will. And yet the will operates and brings about amazing things, as we see everywhere today in the Idealists and in those times in the Pharisees. They are zealous for God, they really are, Paul does not deny it! But in a false way: they set up their own righteousness and scorn the righteousness of God (Rom. 10:2).

There is a corresponding truth in the realm of knowledge. Natural knowledge can show great insight even in the realm of religion (Rom. 1:19-21). This is also true of the revelation of God in Holy Scripture, to which everyone can be privy. Unbelieving scholars can contribute excellent exegetical and also biblically theological insights, which can also be helpful for believers. But, where God is not thereby honoured (Rom. 1:21) there comes a breach which, in the short or long run, causes a falsification of knowledge. Reason governed by the natural will becomes a caricature of revelation. It wants to understand, but not from the starting point of God. Therefore, it must bring its own criteria for understanding and its own models for explaining to the biblical truth.

On the other hand, real knowledge of God's truth and thereby of God himself is possible only when this impeding hostility towards God of the natural man, in other words, sin, is overcome, namely by way of the new birth and conversion (*cf.* 1 Cor. 1:26-30; 2:10-15).

To be sure, conversion in the realm of the mind too is only a *beginning*, even if it is a fundamental one; it must be continued in the ongoing sanctification of the mind (Rom. 12:2; *cf.* 2 Cor. 10:5). 'Be renewed in the spirit of your minds ... and speak the truth' (Eph. 4:23, 25). To speak the truth, to say what corresponds to the truth of God – this is never a matter of course, even for a believing theologian. But it is an ever ongoing possibility when we remain as disciples of Jesus, as disciples of Holy Scripture in the sanctification of our lives and thereby also of our minds.

THE EXPERIENCE OF GUIDANCE BY THE HOLY SPIRIT

SIEGFRIED LIEBSCHNER

By way of introduction it should be said that this essay is not simply a discussion of practical questions (of which there are already quite a number); rather it is more concerned with the biblical and theological questions which are connected with the subject. Further, it concentrates particularly on the guidance of the congregation, a topic which is often neglected alongside the question of personal guidance.

Spiritual Guidance in Evangelical Practice and Literature

The topic is not unknown in the evangelical field in Germany as a whole. As a rule it is taken to be a question of personal guidance and not the experience of being led by the Spirit in a whole church or a group of leaders.

The lives of Spener, Zinzendorf and Tersteegen and a whole series of biographies have contributed to a particular understanding of personal guidance by the Spirit. Nevertheless, this subject does not belong as automatically to being a Christian as does, for example that of conversion. Many Christians neither expect it nor hear anything about it in their churches. Normal experience sets the pattern for life. Others are convinced that God guides their lives in a more general sense and perhaps remember a few particular instances of recognisable guidance. Personal guidance, not only in the major decisions in life but also in the shaping of daily life, seems rather to be a subject for particularly committed Christians.

After the Second World War the subject came into greater prominence through the impetus given by Frank Buchman which has influenced many groups. In the German sphere we may list the SMD (Studenteon Mission in Deutschland), the Marburger Kreis, the

Ruferarbeit, the OJC (Offensive junger Christen), pietistic and independent youth work, etc.

Literature from both the German and the Anglo-Saxon fields shows a large degree of common basic understanding of personal guidance. This basic understanding may be said to have the following characteristics:

1. Spiritual guidance should be the normal experience of every Christian according to God's will.
2. All guidance has to be measured against the words of Scripture.
3. Prayer and meditation are essential if guidance is to be experienced.
4. The experience of guidance can result from direct inspiration.
5. The Spirit of God is revealed to our consciences, our feelings and our thoughts through obstacles or especial clarity and peace with regard to a course of action.
6. The advice of brothers and sisters in the faith is part of guidance, and so too is indeed a life which is open to correction in the fellowship.
7. It is important to pay heed to what circumstances in life have to say.
8. Finally, a wisdom marked by biblical standards and values and a sound commonsense are stressed.

Yet the subject is not so uniformly treated as might now appear. Emphasis may be set on different points, and there are even contradictions. Many people would admit a greater proportion of direct inspirational spiritual guidance. Other people warn against this expectation and stress the dangers of subjectivism and fanaticism. For some people the word of the Bible is almost the only means of spiritual guidance. Fellowship and the advice of fellow Christians play a much lesser role. Dreams, visions and prophecies are usually not mentioned. Other people again are open to these, some because of coming into contact with the charismatic revival, others because of experiences in missionary work among Moslems.

THE EXPERIENCE OF GUIDANCE BY THE HOLY SPIRIT

As examples of opposing points of view the names of J. E. Adams and Klaus Bockmühl can be mentioned. While J. E. Adams, out of fear of subjectivism and disappointments links personal guidance exclusively with the Scriptures, allied with a method of systematic consideration of the different possible courses of action and a test of the conscience, Bockmühl in his writings on ethics and mission argues for the inspirational dimension of spiritual guidance. For example, in the field of ethics this is the way in which the Holy Spirit makes a personal application of God's standards to the individual's own situation. This variety of viewpoints makes theological clarification necessary.

Biblical-Theological Clarifications

In what now follows we will examine three central biblical areas of teaching which say something fundamental about the reality of the Holy Spirit and in particular about guidance through the Spirit.

The Acts of the Apostles has much to say about guidance through the Spirit. The ministry, the mission and the formulation of decisions by the community and its leaders are subject to guidance by the Spirit. The ways in which this is expressed include internal inspiration, the words of one or of several prophets, dreams and visions and even raptures (8:28f., 39; 9:10; 11:27-9; 13:2-4; 16:6f.). The biblical-theological context which is particularly clearly shown by Luke is the sending of the eschatological gift of the Spirit at the appropriate point in salvation history. During the church-age the personal reception of the Spirit is a privilege for the whole church and for every believer (1:8; 2:38). Peter's identification of this event with the promise in Joel 2 shows the Spirit working in a particular way related to guidance and direction (2:17ff.).

In Romans 8 the description of Christian existence which is related to our subject is found in v. 14: 'Those who are led by the Spirit of God are sons of God.' The biblical-theological context of chapters 6 to 8 concentrates on the idea of the Christian life as a life in the Spirit. Verses 12-

16 of chapter 8 show a relationship between a lively personal fellowship and cooperation between the Spirit and us. (E. Brunner describes this using the expression 'person-to-person correspondence'.) The features of this fellowship and cooperation are as follows:
1. The Spirit testifies with our spirit (v. 16).
2. Through the Spirit we address God as father (v. 15).
3. The Spirit leads us (v. 14).
4. Together with the Spirit we put to death the evil deeds of the body (v. 13).

In the final discourses in John's Gospel one of the tasks of the Holy Spirit is to guide into all truth (16:13). On the one hand, the biblical-theological context shows the linking of the Spirit to the sending of Jesus as being central. In the coming of the Spirit the disciples experience again the coming of Jesus and the coming of the Father (14:18, 23). Apart from this nothing is said by the Spirit about himself. On the other hand – and this is of importance in relation to our subject – the context shows the promised permanent indwelling of the Spirit in believers (14:17).

Systematic-Theological Clarifications

A problem arises here. It is true that practical experience and literature often fall short of the biblical level and clarity, but in general they confess the reality of the Spirit who lives in us and wants to guide us. For example, Lausanne 1974 was a living testimony of the dynamic reality of the Spirit who lives and works in contemporary organisations and churches especially in countries in the Third World.

Evangelical theologians share all this more or less as a personal conviction. However, it seems to be difficult to express this reality of the Holy Spirit in theological categories. The Spirit as a constituent characteristic of the new covenant, as the decisive characteristic of Christians, which is thus offered (Acts 2), which is thus awaited (Acts 4:30; 8:15-17), which is counted as an obvious criterion (Acts 15:8f.), about which people inquire (Acts 19:2), of which we are reminded (Gal. 3:2ff.), about which people just know (Acts 5:32; 1 Thes. 4:8; 2 Cor. 1:21f.; and 2 Cor. 11:4), has seldom had, in theological discussion, a clarity comparable with that shown with regard to the revelation of Christ. This is related to the strong Protestant tradition of thought, particularly the Lutheran tradition, in the shadow of which theology is studied especially in Germany. This tradition of thought has seldom been able to disentangle itself from historical questions in teaching on the Holy Spirit (Luther and the Fanatics; the antinomian disputes; the controversy with experience-based piety of a Schleiermachian kind). Usually the biblical passages which were summarised in Part 2 are met with scepticism and warning signs or simply ignored instead of being taken as a challenge to a tired Christianity. The unusual methods of spiritual guidance in the Acts of the Apostles are regarded as intemperate, ambiguous and exotic, while the fellowship with God the Spirit in life and work which is described comes under the terrible suspicion of 'synergism'. The message of the permanent indwelling of the Spirit in believers is most likely to bring warning cries such as 'possession', 'mysticism' and 'subjectivism' into the arena. The danger of understanding the spirit in a naturalistic manner is raised. It ought to be the aim of evangelical theology to teach the reality of the Holy Spirit in a biblical fashion and to point to God's promises. With regard to the problems which occur we must use as our criterion the New Testament itself, particularly Paul, whose teaching on the Holy Spirit is such that all the problems which have appeared up to now, which are our own problems and not those of the Holy Spirit, are given an answer:

firstly by the strict reference to the Christ-event (the Spirit does not proclaim himself but throws light on the Crucified One);

further, by the fact that the Spirit in all its dynamic existence within us is always at one and the same time the Lord and the One who stands over against us, and that his being in us is received only through obedience. That is to

say, expressed in categorical terms: a relationship which is at the same time ontologically real and personal;
then through the relationship of the individual to the fellowship, of the limb to the body;
then through the functioning of the gifts of the Spirit, their character as *diakonia*;
then through the completion of the work of the Spirit in the ethical dimension, with love being the greatest gift;
and, *finally*, by holding fast to the fact that in this age the Spirit and the power of the new world are always merely a beginning and cannot be expected to be perfect.

Paul does this in such a way that, even in Corinth, where the temptation towards a pure 'Word of God' theology would have perhaps been close at hand, he encourages the congregation to take the Holy Spirit into account.

The aim of evangelical theology ought also to be to close the gap between biblical and systematic theology, and to follow the biblical understanding of the Spirit as closely as possible with the language of systematic categories. We have been influenced for centuries by theologies which basically do not think in a trinitarian manner, but sell the revelation short in the classical sketches of the action of God in the life of Christ. By contrast a theology which has an adequate biblical backing against this, is the one which first of all also shows that God the Holy Spirit is making history in us and through us today on the basis of this salvation history. Merely practical instructions are not sufficient for our question or other questions about the reality of the Spirit. There is a need for a theology which bears out the truth of such experience biblically, encourages it, and where necessary corrects it. A definite encouragement towards a theology of this nature is found in Reformed Protestantism, for instance in theologians such as Emil Brunner, A. van Ruler, Rudolph Bohren and Jan Veenhof.

The Experience of Guidance Through the Spirit

1. *Help towards the experiencing of a personal guidance by the Spirit.*

(a) Guidance by the Spirit as part of a total understanding of the Christian life. The literature mentioned above shows more or less quite clearly that guidance by the Spirit is not an isolated subject. In the following I will repeat some typical opinions.

Guidance as the Bible understands it does not begin until after repentance and rebirth, true as it is that God seeks to do the best for the whole of his creation, whether it already obeys him or not.

The time during which guidance is experienced is identical with the time of sanctification, that is to say, when one is ready to place one's life under the Lordship of Jesus.

What belongs above all to the pattern of life as a disciple is the readiness to be moulded in the image of Christ and to accept the word of God as the compulsory framework for personal guidance.

The experience of guidance presupposes that one should not remain in a private way of life in which personal blessing is experienced but should live in readiness for service and mission.

Living under God's guidance is like taking part in a lifelong process in which it is more important to love God in all situations than fearfully to try not to make any mistakes.

When things go properly, then guidance during the normal course of life will become something automatic because we grow closer and closer towards what God intends.

However, guidance will not become 100% experience. We shall have to make decisions which may be right or wrong. Living on the basis of mercy and forgiveness is part of a pilgrimage under the guidance of God.

It is the task of teaching and pastoral work to present guidance by the Spirit as part of such a total picture of life.

(b) The anthropological-psychological aspect of the experience of spiritual guidance. What is meant by this is the influence and colouring due to the individual nature and character of a person. Attention is occasionally drawn to this in literature as a wise piece of advice towards this or that course of action, but in general it is too rarely made the central theme. Pastoral psychology, when it does not follow some human scientific theology but recognises itself to be committed to biblical thinking, can provide help in showing how different types of people with their strengths and weaknesses live under God's guidance. For instance, how should we help an unscrupulous person to live better within God's love and in the present moment? How should we help a person governed by impulses to distinguish between God's will and his own inner demands and fears? How should we help a person who is very self-confident to become more sensitive to divine guidance in a different direction, and so on?

Those involved in pastoral work must become sensitive to particular patterns which have arisen through traditions of piety. For instance, someone may live with a particular recipe for success with God's guidance: expect God's blessings, expect open doors, God is a rich father and he wants to have for himself successful and healthy children. Or somebody lives according to a philosophy in direct contrast to this. The criteria are then somewhat as follows: God's guidance normally goes against your will. He leads you on a hard path because he wants you to bear a cross. Normally God's help comes at the last minute because he wants to test you. Usually you will not understand God's purpose, but it is holy and you must accept it obediently.

What is desirable in all this is not a reorientation of our spiritual teaching and pastoral work towards psychological advice, but a careful combination of insights and observations in a spiritual mould.

2. The guidance of the congregation by the Holy Spirit.

As mentioned earlier, I am going to stress this subject in conclusion, which compared with personal guidance is less well-known. Some people suffer because there is such a large gap between their personal, more or less timid experience of guidance by the Spirit and the level of the creation of a common mind in a group of believers. They suffer because they themselves, despite personal experiences, must suddenly adopt as church leaders, committee members or group leaders, *etc.*, a completely different style, particularly when what is at issue is a question of finance, building or election. Admittedly, this change in the way in which decisions are made is far from becoming apparent to some people.

We are in the fortunate position of recognising two different 'models' which have their place in a fellowship. Not that one is put forward as a spiritual way and the other as a human. Both are experienced as ways followed by the Spirit. In Acts 13 we see the way of prophetic leadership; in Acts 15 the Spirit leads by powerful teaching and by a somewhat tiring path which must be followed by the authorities. Let us follow this brief description with a closer look at these two models, not out of historical interest, but in order that in our search for a framework for spiritual guidance we may find a picture that is laid out in a sufficiently broad and detailed manner.

(a) Guidance through a prophetic word (Acts 13:1-3).
How are we to imagine the whole picture on the basis of the small amount of evidence? The church in Antioch had both prophets and teachers, those who speak by direct inspiration and those who have a better idea of the overall behaviour of God and can sort out and judge individual impulses. The five who are named clearly form the group of church leaders. Paul incidentally is listed last. It is consoling, as one commentator remarks, that even the 'great Paul' started right at the bottom. From the five names,

which all originate from older local churches, we can further conclude that no citizen of Antioch belonged to this circle of leaders, that is to say, no recently converted member of the church. It is clearly a question of people who were already mature followers of the path of guidance by the Spirit.

These five are met together, but whether without or with the rest of the congregation is not revealed in the text. Some kind of meeting of the church leadership is conceivable but different in character from our usual committee meetings. Instead of a businesslike style of meeting a gathering which concentrates its attention on God is meant, as the reference to fasting emphasises.

Accordingly, it is under these conditions, namely the presence of prophets and teachers and the fact that they are gathered together as representatives to concentrate on God, that the Spirit makes his guidance clear and fires the starting gun for the first great phase of mission. Also worthy of notice and of consideration is the fact that it is not Paul and Barnabas themselves who receive a sure sign and then pass on the information to the rest of the astonished gathering. Others declare the great instruction for the pair.

It is definitely the case, for example, that workers in difficult situations can bear greater loads and are calmer if their task is confirmed by a larger group and is not based merely on their own inspiration. Of course it must also be remembered that God had already revealed some of this course of action to Paul beforehand. However, in the decisive hour certainty and commissioning are put on a broad footing. It would be helpful to both parties – workers and the rest of the fellowship – if the spiritual framework was so open that calls to service would come as a happening in the fellowship in a stronger fashion than they do at the moment. Identification and support would profit from it.

It is precisely this which happens here. The church leaders or rather the rest of the church leaders identify themselves strongly with the commissioning of the two men and support it with fasting, prayer and blessing. Perhaps the ability to realise what the Spirit is initiating is also given on account of the fact that this group of leaders have a wide enough horizon. Clearly they lived with an unusual readiness to cross over frontiers. After all, it is no small matter simply to send out two of the most qualified co-workers. Probably they could have done an excellent service in Antioch. I have the impression that we frequently block God's good strategic instructions in that we are hard of hearing when it comes to crossing frontiers. We listen eagerly in favour of the beloved *status quo* and the personal needs of our own church or group. The Spirit of God is not a Spirit of conditions which have been achieved, but a Spirit who is always pursuing further aims with the aid of what has already been achieved. A church or a group of leaders with this basic willingness to move is blessed with good ears for the Spirit's plans.

(b) Guidance by means of a longer path to knowledge (Acts 15). We find ourselves in the same church. One of the great central disputes of early Christianity is being debated. In a small local church situation the question of the freedom of the gospel from the law is decided for the rest of the history of the church of Jesus.

Now for this difficult situation there is no prophecy presented which would have made the process of decision-making considerably shorter. Even the OT – the early church's Bible – cannot simply be opened, for obviously both groups can appeal to it. These remarks show that something must be rejected. Clearly it is not in general right to ask God for direct instructions which will short circuit a long process of enquiry. Clearly it is also not always appropriate to say, 'Let's open the Bible. If we were only to take Scripture seriously, then . . . .' Often after the Bible has been opened the problem is merely made more difficult, because now everybody is armed with good biblical texts. Here a new question which has arisen must rather be dealt with by those with responsibility following a longer, more intensive path to a solution with one another. First of all – in agreement with Romans 12:1f. – the new, relevant way of thinking must be developed. Revelation has been experienced in Christ, but the consequences of this for this new question are not simply readily available.

The path to understanding which is followed has a whole lot of very different parts and phases. Arguments and squabbles are mentioned. Proclamation and reports of God's great deeds among the heathen form part of it. There are phases of discussion, didactic statements of opinion and James' final words of wisdom. This listing is deliberately intended to show the very mixed array of methods. Thus there was not only argument, as is often noted today with a certain satisfaction, in contrast to an earlier interpretation of the passage which liked to play it down. In fact every effort is made so that this hard nut can be cracked. None of the methods is dismissed as wrong; the work of recognition plays a part, and so does discussion for the focussing of new thought, but equally clearly so do the reports of witnesses and the directive comments of individuals.

And yet it is not simply a question of the usual sort of theological discussion. The following points characterise this way of teaching and understanding.

This dispute, no matter what decisive matters depend on it, is not the topic which governs everything else. They get their priorities right on the journey through Samaria, and the same is true in Jerusalem; they make it their business as a first priority to report God's great deeds and not their problem. Our fixation about problems in our dealings and conversation with one another is to my mind a fairly certain way of not resolving the problems. I am not pleading for the suppression of problems, but for the placing of problems in the correct context in our churches, that is to say, the reports of God's doings, both small and great.

Neither is the actual presentation of the case carried out as a tug of war between opinions and arguments, but in such a way that the authorities try on both sides to make each other and themselves aware of the hand of God in the whole situation. What a difference that is whether it is merely the influential opinions of important people that are being exchanged with all the typical temptation to self-opinionatedness in a case of life and death of the individual opinion or whether one, so to speak, always keeps an eye open for the hand of God. Helpful in this are the constantly reintroduced reports of God's working in relation to the problem. What a wealth of learning material for our meetings; this loose integration of serious thought and sticking close to the concrete living works of God.

Finally, this way of finding out God's will includes the silence of the congregation and the speakers about what is reported, the words of wisdom and knowledge of James, the unanimity and finally the certainty that what has been achieved 'is pleasing to the Holy Spirit and to us'. We do not gain the impression that God's Spirit has somehow still managed to get a look in despite a large quantity of pointless individual effort; rather one has the impression that this was precisely the method of the Spirit's guidance.

(c) The necessity for both models of guidance. Thus the Spirit guides us in both ways according as the situation necessitates. In the first case it is a question of accepting a decision of God and following it. With this there is nothing special to learn as regards content, and no grasp of understanding is required. The fact that mission is part of the existence of the church has been learnt in the meantime.

In the second case the problem must first be clearly thought out and viewed. It is not a question of the first method being, as it were, a 'royal way' and the second a 'commoner's way' from which God would like to protect us; it is also not a question of the prophetic method being for beginners who have not yet grown much. Obviously Jesus' church should expect both methods of guidance. The second method is needed because we must first develop

Christlike thinking on many questions. If we limit ourselves and remain 'children in understanding' we will not grasp the inspiration of the Spirit in many questions, or we will reinterpret it and trim it to fit our own level of comprehension. The history of the church of Jesus and the personal history of many Christians and Christian authorities is full of such interpretations of the moving of the Spirit which have turned out to be too brief and too scanty because thought and comprehension were not developed at certain points. God does not simply cut short such proceedings and take care of everything himself, deputising for us as it were. We do not learn anything through that, but on the next similar occasion we behave just as immaturely again. It is then just as necessary that we learn to expect direct guidance and knowledge in times of decision. On the other hand there is precisely as much mature knowledge and experience present in our churches as could be taken up by God's Spirit if we were open to his direct guidance.

Could we envisage that we might learn from these two basic models in our churches:

(1) That we learn to expect direct guidance in meetings of the church leaders.

(2) That groups of leaders come together in a more 'worshipful' way. Helpful experiences are possible in conferences and weekend retreats. In the normal day-to-day life of a church these seem very difficult to attain.

(3) That a particular concentration on listening to God (fasting) may become possible when difficult pastoral questions are being considered or when once again the question of church building is causing problems.

(4) That guidance for others is experienced, and that church and parachurch workers are found through the development of a strongly spiritual understanding. I explained above what opportunities lie in this for both sides.

(5) That we gain the courage to treat central questions of the Christian life, for example, burning ethical question, whereas at present there is sufficient time and interest

during church meetings only for questions of dates, finance and building.

(6) That disputed questions to not confuse priorities and attract all our interest and energy, but that it is precisely then that a fellowship turns first to the living work of God.

(7) That we descend from the style of a Christianly-concealed self-opinionated tug of war and learn the flexibility to pay attention to God's hand, even in what others say....

Could we thus envisage that leaders and church councils and churches would be ready both to reckon with the immediate initiatives of the Spirit and to let themselves be led by God's Spirit into the demanding path of a broadening of their thinking?

3. The significance of spiritual guidance for full-time workers.

I conclude with a challenge to the full-time workers in the church of Jesus, including above all pastors, but also ourselves as theological teachers.

To take seriously the guidance of the Holy Spirit means that we carry out our duties on the basis of listening to God and contact with him. 1 Cor. 1:22ff., 1 Peter 4:11 and also Romans 10:17, which is usually placed in a prominent position, say something about this for our teaching and preaching. This does not exclude either exegesis for preparation in preaching or human psychological help for pastoral work, or an agenda for the church members' meeting or committee meeting, or dictionaries and lexicons for theological work.

Everything should and can be integrated however into a way of living and working based on listening. From the time of preparation until completion we can reckon with the experience of 1 Corinthians 2: 'words' are provided, situations are led by God, those acting on their own authority are hindered. This presupposes openness and the ability to be corrected.It takes for granted that we are at home not only with people and in methods of helping but also in the dimension of the unseen things, which means living and working by prayer and guidance, as for example Paul did to the extent of the experience of 2 Cor. 12:1ff.

To take seriously the guidance of the Holy Spirit means that we reckon with the prophetic elements of authority and certainty.

This is how Paul characterises his work as he looks back in 1 Thessalonians 1:5; 1 Corinthians 2:4; 4:20; 2 Corinthians 10:8. This reckoning with authority and certainty does not mean the end of individual weakness and tendency to err (as far as he himself was concerned, Paul was in fear and trembling when he was with the Corinthians), nor does it mean an 'authoritarian pastoral and leadership style' or a self-opinionated theology; but God's workers themselves and often also their hearers and those who seek advice and students have the remarkable experience that not only do they receive worthwhile opinions and advice but that God speaks. that he meets the need of specific families, groups and churches, and that what is now necessary for Jesus' church is what is taught.

Often such a type of service and work under real guidance from Jesus begins when we renew our previously experienced calling and commissioning after many years.

TOWARDS A BIBLICAL THEOLOGY OF EXPERIENCE

KLAAS RUNIA

Introduction

The question, What is the place of experience in our Christian life and in our theology?, is of tremendous *importance*. Most Christians intuitively realize that it is not enough to have an intellectual knowledge of the Christian faith, but that it must be accompanied by experience. Young people in particular are very sensitive at this point. They are not satisfied with religion as a formal ritual obligation but ask :What does it mean to you? How does it function in your own life? What kind of experience does it produce?

I believe these are very relevant questions and fully in conformity with Scripture. It may be true that the *term* 'experience' does not occur much in Scripture (as a matter of fact, the term is mentioned only three times in Cruden's Concordance), but the reality of experience is found everywhere, especially in the Psalms, in the writings of the prophets and in the New Testament Epistles. We also notice in the history of the Christian Church that in times of revival there were clear manifestations of the Holy Spirit, which produced deep experiences.

At the same time both the Bible and the history of the Christian Church also teach us that we have to be careful with experiences. One thing in particular we have to guard against, namely, that personal experience becomes our only spiritual guide, for then we would land into pure subjectivism and theologically we would arrive at a 'theology of experience', in which the religious consciousness of pious man becomes the source of theological knowledge (*cf.* the theology of Schleiermacher and his followers, and the psychology of religion as espoused by men such as William James).

As I said before, pure doctrine is not enough, *we also need experience*. But the reverse is also true: pure experience is not enough, *we also need sound doctrine*. In his book, *Dynamics of Spiritual Life, An Evangelical Theology of Renewal*, Richard Lovelace has pointed out that the revivals of Billy Sunday were real and powerful manifestations of the Holy Spirit, but that they also 'produced Christians who were shallow, moralistic and culture-bound.'[1] Our experience must be constantly checked and controlled by the objective Word of God. Our mind too must be renewed and illuminated by the Holy Spirit. Lovelace also points out that according to Ronald Knox 'the neglect of rationality is a prime example of the central error of all enthusiasm.'[2]

We must also be careful not to confuse experience with *emotion*. Undoubtedly, the emotional element is very essential to experience, but the two are not simply identical. Actually experience is a very broad concept. Harold Kuhn points out that the term as such includes all our conscious processes. 'It involves sense perceptions, feelings, memory, recollections, knowledge, prejudices, illusions, hopes, fears, beliefs, etc.'[3] It is therefore also necessary to take the concept of Christian experience in a broader sense than is often done. I find Kuhn's own definition, as given in the same article, too narrow: 'the conscious reception of the ministry of divine grace in the life of the soul'. The last words in particular tend to limit Christian experience to the 'mystical' aspect only. But in reality it is much wider; it embraces the whole life of the Christian, not only his feel-

1. *Op. cit.* (1979), p. 262. Lovelace's book is one of the best recent studies about the value and the dangers of experience.
2. *Op. cit.*, p. 265.
3. Harold B. Kuhn, 'Experience', *Baker's Dictionary of Theology* (1960), p. 207. This broad conception of experience is increasingly becoming popular in present-day theology. *Cf.*, *e.g.*, Edward Schillebeeck, *Christ, The Christian Experience in the Modern World* (1980), pp. 30ff.; Walter Kasper, *Glaube im Wandel der Geschichte* (1970), pp. 132ff.

ings and the stirrings of his soul, but also his thinking and his actions.

I was happy to notice that Lovelace also uses a much broader concept. Taking his starting point in the union with Christ he discusses at length the many 'dimensions of experience' that issue from this union and that can be appropriated by faith and sought for in the life of the church. He admits that it is not an easy matter. At first such an inquiry seems to transcend all analysis. 'It is like a blaze of white light which contains an almost numberless succession of colours and wavelengths, "the unsearchable riches of Christ, ... the manifold wisdom of God" (Eph. 3:8,10).'[4] But when he starts to analyse it, a whole series of different colours becomes visible, and they appear to embrace the whole existence of the Christian.[5]

The Source of Christian Experience

The *source* of experience is our *union with Christ*. But how does this union come about? The answer of Scripture is: this is the *work of the Holy Spirit*. Already in the Old Testament we read about the divine promise that in the last days God will pour out his Spirit upon all flesh (Joel 2:28). In his conversation with the Samaritan woman Jesus says that 'whoever drinks of the water that I shall give him will never thirst; the water that I shall give him will become in him a spring of water welling up to eternal life' (John 4:14). Later on, on the last day of the feast of Tabernacles, Jesus proclaims: 'If any one thirst, let him come to me and drink. He who believes in me, as the scripture has said, "Out of his heart shall flow rivers of living water"' (John 7:37,38). In his comment John adds that Jesus said this about the Spirit which those who be-

4. *Op. cit.*, p. 74.
5. See the chart, *op.cit.*, p. 75, where four primary elements (justification, sanctification, the indwelling Spirit, authority in spiritual conflict) and five secondary elements (mission, prayer, community, disenculturation, theological integration) are mentioned.

lieved in him were to receive (v. 39). After his resurrection Jesus charges his disciples to wait for the promise of the Father, for before many days they will be baptized with the Holy Spirit (Acts 1:4f). On the day of Pentecost this promise is fulfilled. All believers present in Jerusalem are 'filled with the Holy Spirit' (Acts 2:4).

This coming of the Spirit is an altogether new event in the series of God's saving acts. The Spirit 'creates a world of his own, a world of conversion, experience, sanctification; of tongues, prophecy, and miracles; of mission; of upbuilding and guiding the church, etc. He appoints ministers; he organizes; he illumines, inspires, and sustains; he intercedes for the saints and helps them in their weaknesses; he searches everything, even the depths of God; he guides into all truth; he grants a variety of gifts; he convinces the world; he declares the things that are to come. In short, as the Johannine Jesus says: "he who believes in me will also do the works that I do; and greater works than these will he do, because I go to the Father"(14:12)'.[6]

All this means that the doctrine of experience actually is part of the doctrine of the Holy Spirit. We must even say more: it is not just a part, but the very centre of the doctrine of the Holy Spirit. It is therefore no wonder that groups and movements that were looking for Christian experience always concentrated on the work of the Spirit. We observe that throughout the history of the Christian Church, from the Montanists in the second century to the Pentecostal and Charismatic Movements in our own century. Usually these groups and movements reacted against the lack of spiritual reality in the life of the official church. Rightly they tried to correct this by centring all their attention on the Spirit and his work. But as so often happens in reaction movements, they were usually inclined to over-react. In the first place, they tended to make the

---

6. Hendrikus Berkhof, *The Doctrine of the Holy Spirit* (1964), p. 23.

Spirit an independent centre of new actions. Secondly, they tended to concentrate one-sidedly on what happens in the believer himself. The result of the first tendency is that Jesus Christ and his work easily recede into the background. The result of the second tendency may easily be that the difference between God's Spirit and man's spirit becomes blurred.

But such tendencies are in contrast with what we find in Scripture itself. In the New Testament the Holy Spirit is always and everywhere the *Spirit of Christ*. 'There is no reference in the New Testament of any work of the Spirit apart from Christ. The Spirit is, in an exclusive sense, the Spirit of Christ.'[7] The whole work of the Spirit can be summarized in his action of bringing us into union with Christ, so that *we* are in Christ but that *Christ* is also in us. First he convinces us that Jesus Christ is the Saviour and that we owe our whole salvation to him. Then, he makes ours in experience all the benefits that Jesus has acquired for us in his saving work and makes us his witnesses in this world. In this connection H. J. Wotherspoon has used the image of stained glass. The Spirit 'reaches us through the Lord Jesus, as the light shines into the Temple through the pictured glass, the same light that pours from the sun, but coloured by the medium through which it passes, and carrying to the wall on which it now falls the image of the figure through which it shines. So the Holy Spirit reaches us, tinged as it were, by the nature through which He is mediated to us, indistinguishable in character from the soul of the Lord Himself, bearing to us His thoughts, His emotions, His impulses, impressing upon us His will, permeating our being with His vitality.'[8] For the very same reason there can be no blurring of the difference between God's spirit and our own spirit. Everything that is not in

---

7. George S. Hendry, *The Holy Spirit in Christian Theology* (1957), p. 26.
8. H. J. Wotherspoon, *What Happened at Pentecost* (1937), p. 36.

conformity with Christ is not from the Spirit of God but from our own spirit.

This also provides us with a clear and firm *criterion* for both our experience itself and our doctrine of experience. In both cases the fundamental question is: Does it glorify Christ? In his Paraclete sayings Jesus himself has stated it quite clearly that the Spirit bears witness to him, glorifies him, and takes his things in order to declare them to us (John 15:26; 16:13f). Does our experience glorify Christ or does our emphasis on experience actually squeeze him out of the picture and concentrate on what *we* see in ourselves and what *we* feel as the actions of the Spirit in our own souls? Authentic Christian experience points to Jesus Christ and to his work. Fullness of the Spirit can only mean that we are full of Christ and of his salvation and of his obedience to the Father. This is also the way to become sure of the presence of the Spirit in our lives. W. H. Griffith Thomas once received a letter from a woman, saying: 'I have prayed, I have read the Bible, I have striven. I have done all that I can and I still am not sure whether I have the fullness of the Spirit.' Thomas's reply was: 'Turn your thoughts out, not in. What is Christ to you? If He is little you have not the fullness of the Spirit. If He is Chief among ten thousand and Altogether Lovely, you have the fullness of the Spirit.'[9] Another way of putting it is: 'The Spirit of Jesus is the Spirit which marked him out as Son of God, as Servant of Yahweh, and sent him on his mission to Israel and the world. If the Spirit of Jesus is the gift bestowed on his followers, we shall expect to find the same characteristics marking authentic Christian life in the Spirit.'[10]

In the last quotation we read that the Spirit is the gift bestowed on the followers of Jesus Christ. That means that *all believers receive the Holy Spirit*. We find this throughout the whole New Testament. We hear it in Jesus'

---

9. Told by Leon Morris, *Spirit of the Living God* (1960), p. 66.
10. Michael Green, *I Believe in the Holy Spirit* (1977), p. 54.

own exclamation on the feast of Tabernacles: *'He who believes in me*, as the scripture has said, "Out of his heart shall flow rivers of living water"' (John 7:38). On the day of Pentecost 'they were *all* filled with the Holy Spirit' (Acts 2:4). In his sermon on that very same day Peter says that 'everyone whom the Lord our God calls to him' shall receive the gift of the Holy Spirit (Acts 2:39f.). According to Paul all the members of the congregation were by one Spirit baptized into one body and all were made to drink of one Spirit (1 Cor. 12:13; *cf.* also Rom. 5:5; 8:9-11; 1 Cor. 6:19; 2 Cor. 5:5; 1 Thess. 4:7). When a person comes to faith he receives the gift of the Spirit. Of course, his coming to faith is already the work of the Spirit. But that is not the end of it. It always issues in the reception of the Spirit as a permanent gift.

The new believer will also *experience the gift.* That does not mean that it will always break forth in him as the water of a fast moving creek. That depends on the way in which we come to faith. Some people go through a deep crisis. In the life of others it is more a matter of growth by degrees. In the first case the conversion is a high water mark, accompanied by strong experience. In the second case it is a gradual growth into ever deepening experience. But whatever the case may be, there will be experience of the presence of the Spirit.

Two Stages in Christian Experience
In the Christian Church there have again and again been people who adopted the idea of a two-stage experience. (a) There would be the initial gift of the Spirit to all believers. (b) There would be a subsequent gift of the Spirit to those who seek for it. This idea has been expressed in various ways. John Wesley called the subsequent gift the gift of Christian perfection (entire sanctification). Charles Finney spoke of the doctrine of full justification. R. A. Torrey called it the baptism with the Spirit and Andrew Murray propagated the doctrine of the indwelling

Spirit.[11] Modern day Pentecostals and Charismatics speak of the baptism with the Spirit, accompanied by speaking in tongues.[12] In all cases it means a new quality of Christian experience distinct from conversion and it usually means that the new experience makes Christian living at the previous level look 'so pale and shoddy that it is hardly worthy of the name Christian at all.'[13]

Behind this idea of a two-stage experience we can distinguish *several reasons*. First, there is the unsatisfactory situation in the spiritual life of many believers. Lovelace describes it as follows: 'The typical relationship between believers and the Holy Spirit in today's church is too often like that between the husband and wife in a bad marriage. They live under the same roof, and the husband makes constant use of his wife's services, but he fails to communicate with her, recognize her presence and celebrate his relationship with her.'[14] Secondly, when people begin to realize their situation they begin to long for more and deeper experience. When they read their Bible they see that this must be possible. Does the apostle Paul not speak of the 'fullness' of the Spirit? Thirdly, there are certain passages in the New Testament that seem to speak clearly of such a two-stage experience. Texts that speak of the fullness of the spirit, of sealing with the Spirit, of baptism with the Spirit, all seem to speak of an 'extra', a 'plus', that may be given after conversion. Especially certain passages from the Acts of the Apostles (Acts 8, Acts 9, Acts 10 and 11 and Acts 19) play an important role in this discussion. In particular the first two and the last are

---

11. *Cf.* Frederick Dale Bruner, *A Theology of the Holy Spirit* (1970), pp. 323ff.
12. It is interesting to note that Catholic theologians, such as Thornton, Mason and Gregory Dix, also adopt a two-stage initiation, namely, water baptism and the imposition of hands in confirmation. *Cf.* Green, *op. cit.*, p. 125.
13. Green, *op.cit.*, p. 126.
14. Lovelace, *op.cit.*, p. 131.

seen to distinguish between coming to faith and receiving a special measure of the Spirit.

Nevertheless, I believe that we have to be very careful here. Luke does not offer us a 'theology of Christian initiation'. It is impossible to distinguish a clear theological 'scheme' in all these passages. His aim is not to develop his own theology (although he undoubtedly had an astute theological mind), but he wants to describe the history of the young church and in doing this simply tells us what happened on various occasions. And then there appears a great variety of experiences. 'Sometimes reception of the Spirit follows baptism (e.g. Acts 2:28ff); sometimes it precedes baptism (e.g. Acts 10:44-48); and sometimes a man is baptised who has no part or lot in the Christian thing, and whose heart is still fast bound in wickedness (Acts 8:21).'[15] In the cases of Paul's conversion of the twelve disciples at Ephesus and the Samaritan converts it is different again.[16] It should further be noted that in the New Testament itself the expression 'baptism with the Spirit' is never applied to a second experience. It is used seven times. Six times it refers to the contrast between John the Baptist who baptized with water and Jesus who baptizes with the Holy Spirit and with fire (matt. 3:11; Mark 1:8; Luke 3:16; John 1:33; Acts 1:5 and 11:16). The only other time that the expression is used it refers to the baptism of *all* believers (I Cor. 12:13). I think Fr Killian McDonnell is right when he concludes that 'to be baptised in the Holy Spirit' is simply another scriptural way of saying 'to receive the Holy Spirit'.[17]

Yet the matter is not solved by the interpretation of a handful of Bible texts. The *problem* to which it refers remains, namely, that so many believers experience so little, while some have a much richer experience. I believe that this fact has to be recognized and to be taken seriously.

---

15. Green, *op.cit.*, p. 133.
16. *Cf.* Green, *op.cit.*, pp. 134ff.
17. Quoted in Green, *op.cit.*, p. 146.

But there is not sufficient evidence to seek the solution in the way of a doctrine of a two-stage experience. The doctrinal teaching of the New Testament, as we find it in particular in Paul's epistles, is that the gift of the Spirit is so rich that all believers must continually seek for a *deepening* of the work of the Spirit in his own life. So Paul writes to the Ephesians: 'Be filled with the spirit' (6:18). He uses the present imperative. Now this process can take place in various manners. It may be in the form of a growth pattern or follow a crisis pattern. But this is not really essential. Both patterns should be looked upon as authentic ways of realizing the grace of the Spirit at the conscious level.[18] In either case no party should look down upon the other. At any rate, those who reject the idea of a two-stage experience should ask themselves: 'Have we that power in prayer, that strength over temptation, that growing Christ-likeness, which marked the communities of Christ in New Testament days and of which the one baptism was the outward bond?'[19]

Growth in Christian Experience

Another question that must be faced is: *How do we grow into the fullness of the Spirit*? Does it mean that we have to fulfil certain *conditions*? This idea is often related to the doctrine of a two-stage experience. In the Appendix of his book *A Theology of the Holy Spirit*, where he briefly mentions the views of John Wesley, Charles Finney, R. A. Torrey and Andrew Murray, Frederick Bruner clearly shows how they all set certain conditions that have to be met in order to reach the second stage of the experience. Throughout his entire book this also appears to be true of the Pentecostal doctrine. As such this is not new. Luther noticed this already in Karlstadt. In 1525 he wrote: 'With all (his) mouthing of the words, "Spirit, Spirit, Spirit", he tears down the bridge, the path, the way, the ladder, and

---

18. *Cf.* Green, op. cit., p. 146.
19. Green, *op. cit.*, p. 147.

all the means by which the Spirit might come to you. Instead of the outward order of God in the material sign of baptism and the oral proclamation of the Word of God he wants to teach you not how the Spirit comes to you but how you come to the Spirit.'[20]

Here too we have to be very careful indeed. We have to guard against the danger that faith becomes a meritorious work. Bruner's whole study is aimed against this danger. He rightly points out that Paul always contrasts faith with 'the works of the law'.[21] Whatever faith may be, it can never be a 'work'. Faith is not something that issues from man toward God, but it emanates from the Gospel to the human recipient. Faith is to say Yes to the offer of the Gospel. Faith is the empty hand in which we receive the riches of God's grace. Bruner puts it thus: 'Faith is the receptacle of Christ. Where there is faith in Christ, there Christ is in faith. That is simply the gospel.'[22] I fully agree with this. And yet, this is not all that is to be said here.

When a person has come to faith, when he has accepted Jesus Christ as his Saviour and has received the gift of the Spirit, this person is immediately *co-responsible* for his own spiritual life. This is the essential difference between the doctrine of Christ and the doctrine of the Spirit. In the *Christology* man is utterly passive. Christ does everything for him, without him. In the *Pneumatology* man is no longer passive but he is immediately employed by the Spirit. The Spirit takes man, with his whole personality, into his service and makes him responsible for his own spiritual life. Unfortunately, there is much misplaced passivity at this point. Many believers think that the Spirit has to do it all and that they themselves can do nothing else than wait for the Spirit to stir them into action. But this is definitely not true. 'It is our privilege and responsibility, to speak, to drive the car, and by our own deliberate and sustained

---

20. Bruner, *op.cit.*, 231. *Cf.* Luther, *LW* 40, p. 147.
21. Bruner, *op.cit.*, p. 246
22. Bruner, *op.cit.*, p. 233.

choice to direct it uphill and not down. For God's gift to us of new life in Christ makes this actively possible on our part, as it never was before.'[23]

But even so it remains a matter of faith, and never becomes a matter of 'synergism'. *Synergism* is wrong not only in the Christology but also in the doctrine of the Holy Spirit. Synergism here would mean that we complement the work of the Spirit. It also means that, because we do so much, we can, as it were, force the Spirit to do his part. Synergism makes man an independent factor in the spiritual process. It is always a matter of 50-50, or, if we are a little more humble, of 90-10 or even 99-1. But in each case we, as it were, take over part of the Spirit's work. But this is not true, not even in the doctrine of the Spirit.

The relationship is quite different. The Spirit expects us to do the full 100%, while he at the same time does his 100%. That does not make it 200%, but together it remains 100%. It is entirely his work and it is entirely our work, but each on his own level. As Berkhof put it: 'We do not cooperate with God on the same level, but we operate through him and under him.'[24] In the seventeenth century the authors of the *Canons of Dort* expressed it thus: 'He moves and strengthens the will in such a way that as a good tree it can bear fruits of good works. . . . And so the will, now being renewed, is not only carried and moved by God, but, moved by God, it also works itself. That is why we rightly say that man, by the grace which he has received, believes and converts' (III, par. 11 and 12). The Canons refer here to the conversion and coming to faith of a man. But the same is true of the whole spiritual life of the Christian: *moved by God, he himself now moves!*

---

23. A. M. Stibbs and J. I. Packer, *The Spirit Within You* (1967), p. 50.
24. Berkhof, *op.cit.*, p. 72.

Justification and Christian Experience

The next question we have to ask is: *What* do we experience? What is the *content* of Christian experience? The Bible uses a plethora of terms and expressions here. We read of regeneration, cleansing, illumination, conversion, faith, justification, sanctification, Christ in us, the Spirit in us, abundant life, filling with the Spirit, *etc*. It should be noted that in the New Testament these terms are nearly always used in a non-technical sense and that they often indicate the entire work of the Spirit. At times they also overlap. If we want to get a proper view of all this riches, we have to systematize it and put it into certain clusters, choosing a main heading for each cluster. In the following we shall deal with three main clusters.

There is quite a cluster of experiences that are related to *justification by faith*. According to Brunner justification is the heart of the New Testament Gospel. He even says: 'God's justification of the sinner is the meaning of the New Testament.'[25] I wholeheartedly agree with this, but would like to add that this justification is not without experience. It is not a theoretical insight only, a matter of pure *assensus* or intellectual *notitia*, but when a person is justified something happens not only *to* him but also *in* him. The 'objective' never remains purely 'objective' but is always accompanied by its 'subjunctive' revelation.[26]

What is this *subjective revelation*? It contains several aspects, which we shall put in a certain order. We do not want to suggest by this that this is the exact systematic order, still less that it is a chronological order. They all belong together, so much so that the one is never present without the other

1. There is the *conviction of sin*. This conviction is not a natural, spontaneous thing in man. Natural man is willing to admit faults, mistakes and errors; he also has a sense

---

25. Bruner, *op.cit.*, p. 234.
26. *Cf. Ibid.*, p. 269.

of guilt, both psychologically and existentially. But a real conviction of sin is possible only when we are confronted with the majesty and holiness of God, as this is manifested in the cross of Christ. Only then we acquire a deep sense of our own unworthiness.

2. This will lead to the *confession of our sin*. In shame we bow before this holy God and confess our unworthiness. If our conviction is really deep, our confession will be very concrete. We say with David: 'I know my transgressions, and my sin is ever before me' (Ps. 51:3).

3. But this confession is *never without hope*, for we have found *Jesus Christ* as the Lamb of God that takes away the sin of the world and we put all our trust in him and his great sacrifice on the cross. We believe that this sacrifice was also the expiation and propitiation for our sins (1 John 2:2).

4. Because of this faith in Christ we obtain the *assurance* that God accepts us and forgives our sins. We obtain the assurance of peace with God, of having been adopted into his family as his sons and daughters (Gal. 4:6; Rom. 8:15-17). This assurance is not an extra, but belongs to the very essence of faith. James Denney once called it the touchstone of any version of Christianity. He illustrated this by saying that, whereas in conventional Catholicism it is a sin, and in conventional Protestantism it is a duty, in the New Testament assurance is simply a *fact*.[27]

5. Along this way we are also brought into a *new freedom*. We are no longer slaves of sin and death, of the law and condemnation by the law, of the laws and traditions of men, but we are free children of God. Paul speaks of the 'glorious liberty of the children of God' (Rom. 8:21), and

---

27. Stibbs and Packer, *op.cit.*, p. 87.

that is no wonder, for 'where the Spirit of the Lord is, there is freedom' (2 Cor. 3:17).

Sanctification and Christian Experience

A second cluster of experiences is related to *sanctification*, which not only follows justification but is also quite different from it. Not in the sense that, contrary to justification, sanctification would mean that we ourselves have to do it in our own Christian strength. Berkhof rightly points out that it is *one movement of the Spirit.* 'We are dealing with one and the same movement. God's word is always a creative act. In calling us his sons, he makes us behave as sons. In creating a new relation, he creates a new being. It is really one twofold grace. In that one grace, justification and sanctification are not two parts; in the one event they are related as fundament and goal, as root and fruit.'[28]

The New Testament teaches quite clearly that our sanctification is also *in Jesus Christ.* God made him not only our righteousness, but also our sanctification (1 Cor. 1:30). In his name we have been sanctified (1 Cor. 6:11 — note the Aorist!). In his sacrifice on the cross He has also sanctified us (Eph. 5:26 — again the Aorist!). But what about our good works? Are not they our own achievement? Paul's reply is: 'We are his (*i.e.*, God's) workmanship, created in Christ Jesus for good works, which God prepared beforehand, that we should walk in them' (Eph. 2:10). Our whole sanctification comes from Christ through the Holy Spirit. Therefore the New Testament can call the believers 'saints' (*hagioi*) or 'those who are sanctified' (*hagiasmenoi, cf.* Heb. 10:14; Acts 20:32; 26:18; *etc.*).

At the same time the effectuation of this given sanctification in our own personal lives takes place in the form of a continuous process, and in this process we ourselves are involved. Again we must say that the Spirit *employs us with all our possibilities and capabilities.* And so Paul can

---

28. Berkhof, *op.cit.*, p. 74.

write to the Corinthians: 'Since we have these promises, beloved, let us cleanse ourselves from every defilement of body and spirit, and make holiness perfect in the fear of God' (2 Cor. 7:1). 'The fact that holiness can be "perfected" shows that it is progressive in its nature. Throughout the whole of our lives we are engaged in an activity of defeating sin, and producing righteousness.'[29]

What do we experience in this process? Again I can only give some indications and again I want to stress that the order given does not mean a fixed systematic, still less a chronological order.

1. In the first place there will be a *deepening conviction of sin*, as E. F. Kevan has said: 'The more sanctified a man is, the more will he acknowledge the wretchedness of his own heart. This is the saving work of the Holy Spirit: this is the deepening conviction of sin without which no man shall be sanctified.'[30]

2. Secondly, we will begin not only to *hate sin* but also to *fight against it*. Sanctification means a struggle with our own flesh, that is, with sin in ourselves. The New Testament speaks here of mortifying or putting to death the deeds of the body (Rom. 8:13) and of crucifying the flesh with its passions and desires (Gal. 5:24).

3. But this struggle not only has a 'negative' side. There is also the experience of the *power of the Spirit* who enables us to *conquer the flesh*. There is also the experience of the truth of the promises: 'Resist the devil and he will flee from you' (James 4:7). Leon Morris tells the story of a drunkard who was converted and who later met some of his mates. Their reaction was: 'You don't mean to tell us that you believe in the Bible! Do you really think that Jesus changed water into wine?' 'Well, I don't know about that', the man

---

29. Morris, *op.cit.*, p. 85.
30. E. F. Kevan, *The Saving Work of the Spirit* (1953), p. 24.

said, 'but I do know that in my house He has changed beer into furniture!' The struggle with sin in sanctification is not a vain struggle. 'If the Spirit of him who raised Jesus from the dead dwells in you, he who raised Christ Jesus from the dead will give life to your mortal bodies also through the Spirit which dwells in you' (Rom. 8:11).

4. Do we also experience the *fruit of the Spirit*, as mentioned in Gal. 5:22f. – 'love, joy, peace, patience, kindness, goodness, faithfulness, gentleness, self-control?' One could call this a description of a *Christian character*. Michael Green calls it 'the Spirit of Christ-likeness', for what is it but a description of the character of Jesus himself?[31] It is striking that most of the things mentioned here are aimed at the *neighbour* (as, of course, was also the case with Jesus!). For this reason I think that this fruit is primarily something that *others* will experience in their dealings with us rather than that it is a matter of our own experience (even though it will not be altogether outside our own experience). A truly sanctified person will not think highly of himself. In fact, that would be exactly contrary to the fruit of the Spirit! Let others experience this, as long as we ourselves clearly remember what Frederick Bruner says: 'The *test*, the *evidence* of authentic spirituality according to John was, in a word, love and not special experience.'[32]

5. What we do experience is the *joy* that the life in the Spirit imparts. Again and again the New Testament tells us about the early Christians that they were filled with joy. On the very day of Pentecost they apparently were so happy and merry, even hilarious, that others accused them of being full of new wine! Even persecution did not destroy this joy. On the contrary, we read that they were filled with joy and with the Holy Spirit (Acts 13:52). If joy is

---

31. Green, *op.cit.*, pp. 88ff.
32. Bruner, *op.cit.*, p. 276.

lacking in our life, we do not have the religion of the New Testament.

6. Do we also experience the *guidance of the Spirit*? I believe we do, but I also believe that we have to understand it properly. Guidance by the Spirit is not just a voice from heaven, nor is it a matter of opening your Bible at random and then take as the message the first text you read. If we seek for the guidance of the Spirit, we have to open our hearts for the total message of Scripture, give our serious attention to the circumstances in which we find ourselves and listen to the advice of our fellow-Christians. Along this way the Spirit will make it gradually clear to us what we must do.

7. Finally, we will also experience that he urges us to engage in *prayer* and that he gives power to our prayers. But also, when we do not know what to ask for, we will experience his presence in us and apperceive that He prays in and with us and at times puts the words into our hearts and mouths.

The Gifts of the Spirit and Christian Experience

Justification and sanctification, however, are not the complete work of the Spirit. There is still a *third* work, namely, his giving of 'charismata' (Rom. 12:6-8; 1 Cor. 12:8-10; 12:28-30; Eph. 4:11; 1 Pet. 4:10,11). Some of them are rather spectacular (speaking in tongues, miracles, healings); others look more like ordinary human abilities (utterance of wisdom, utterance of knowledge, ability to distinguish between spirits); others again are somewhere between the spectacular and the ordinary (prophecy, service). But of whatever kind they may be, the New Testament ascribes them all to the Spirit as his special gifts.

Are they also a matter of *experience*? This is undoubtedly true of some of them. He who speaks in tongues knows that he is speaking to God and utters mysteries in the Spirit (1 Cor. 12:2,3). Those who claim to have received this gift tell us that they experience a deep joy in the Spirit. Likewise he who prophesies knows that he speaks through the Spirit and thus he experiences the presence of the Spirit. Whether this is also true of the less spectacular, the more 'ordinary' gifts I do not know. What I do know is that nearly all gifts of the Spirit are not primarily directed at the believer himself but at the *congregation* or the *world*. In the book of Acts, the book of the mission of the Church, the emphasis is on the communication of the Gospel to those who do not yet know it: 'People begin to prophesy, to exclaim, to praise God, to be Christ's witnesses, to speak in tongues, to testify to the enemies, to speak the Word of God with boldness, to proclaim Jesus.'[33] In Paul's writings the emphasis is on the edification of the congregation (1 Cor. 14; Rom. 12). The only gift that centres on the believer himself, speaking in tongues, comes last in his list of charismata in 1 Cor. 12 (vv. 19 and 30). Paul does not disparage it; he even says: 'I want you all to speak in tongues' (1 Cor. 14:5); but in the context of church and world are the other gifts that are not self-orientated more important, for they have the aim of edifying the congregation (1 Cor. 14:5) or of convicting the unbelievers (1 Cor. 14:24, 25).

People in the *charismatic movement* usually go much further. In a review of Berkhof's book *The doctrine of the Holy Spirit* W. W. Verhoef wrote that the charismatic aspect of the work of the Spirit has far-reaching consequences for a person's experience of faith. The gift of the Spirit adds a surprising and profound dimension to this experience. The believer is intensely and concretely involved in this work and he experiences this too. This view of Verhoef is based on the assumption that the charismatic aspect is additional to faith and given in a second, post-conversion experience. As I have stated before, I do not believe that this is the teaching of the New Testament. As

---

33. Berkhof, *op.cit.*, p. 89.

far as I understand the New Testament, it teaches us that every believer receives one or more gifts from the Spirit, when he comes to faith in Christ. This is the teaching of 1 Cor. 12:7 and 11 and also the presupposition of Rom. 12:6-8 and 1 Pet. 4:10. I therefore believe that our real problem is not that we never received a gift and must seek for it, but rather that we have never given proper attention to it and therefore have *neglected the gift* bestowed upon us. This may well be the reason that there is such a lack of missionary zeal in many a congregation. Lovelace rightly points out that it is not enough for us to concentrate on personal sanctification. 'A church which is pursuing personal sanctification is not necessarily one which is powerfully effective in mission, as the Puritans found. There is an additional dimension of waiting upon the Spirit for missionary outreach which is necessary to transcend a self-oriented individualistic piety and begin to carry out the acts of the risen Lord.'[34] But even such 'corporate waiting' may not be our first task. Our first task may well be that within the congregation we help each other to *discover* the gift(s) allotted to us. For it is only through the use of the gifts that we can become a truly live and a truly mission-minded congregation. The gifts will enable us to express and communicate in some way our knowledge of Christ and his grace.[35] At the same time we ourselves will increasingly experience the activity of the Spirit in our own lives. But this experience will not (or no longer) be aimed primarily at ourselves but at others. Stibbs and Packer rightly say 'that the true use of gifts is bound up, not with self-display, party spirit, or any "holier-than-thou" complex, but with self-effacing, loving service of others for our Saviour's sake.'[36]

In 1 Cor. 12 two very clear *tests* are given with regard to the charismata and also with regard to the claims people

---

34. Lovelace, *op.cit.*, p. 125.
35 *Cf.* Stibbs and Packer, *op.cit.*, p. 63.
36. *Ibid.*, p. 66.

TOWARDS A BIBLICAL THEOLOGY OF EXPERIENCE

make in this respect. The first test we find in verse 3. We must ask: 'Does the gift point unmistakably to Jesus as Lord?' The second we find in verse 7. Here we must ask, 'Does the gift serve the common good of the congregation?' A third test can be derived from 1 Cor. 14:24, 25. 'Does the gift serve the mission of the church and does it enable the recipient to lead other people to Christ?' Furthermore, we may never forget that *1 Corinthians 13* stands in between 1 Corinthians 12 and 14. In his *A Plain Account of Christian Perfection* John Wesley writes: 'Another ground of these, and a thousand mistakes, is the not considering deeply that love is the highest gift of God – humble, gentle, patient love; that all visions, revelations, manifestations whatever, are little things compared to love; and that all the gifts above mentioned are either the same with it or infinitely inferior to it. It would be well you should be thoroughly sensible of this – the heaven of heavens is love. There is nothing higher in religion – there is, in effect, nothing else; if you look for anything but more love, you are looking wide of the mark, you are getting out of the royal way. And when you are asking others, "Have you received this or that blessing?", if you mean anything but more love, you mean wrong; you are leading them out of the way, and putting them upon a false scent. Settle it in your heart, that... you are to aim at nothing more, but more of that love described in the thirteenth of Corinthians. You can go no higher than this till you are carried into Abraham's bosom.'[37]

Conclusions

Here on earth experience will always remain limited. Even its high-water marks are not yet the fullness. However deep our experiences may be, they are still no more than a foretaste of what is to come. The perfect filling with the Spirit will be at the *consummation* of all things. The New Testament makes that quite clear by the way in which it

---

37. Quoted from Green, *op.cit.*, pp. 121f.

speaks of the Spirit. On the one hand, it calls him the *'aparche'*, the first fruits (Rom. 8:23). That means the Spirit himself, as we experience him now with all his gifts, is only the beginning of the full harvest that will come at the consummation. On the other hand, it also calls him the *arrabon*, the first instalment, the downpayment (2 Cor. 1:22; 5:5; Eph. 1:14). Basically it is the same idea. The Spirit, given to us, is a foretaste of the final inheritance. At the same time, however, the word also indicates that the inheritance itself is much greater. What we experience here is 'only a *small fraction* of the future endowment'.[38] What the consummation itself will be like we cannot even imagine. Then our whole being and our whole existence will be filled by the Spirit. In 1 Cor. 15 (:44) Paul speaks of the 'spiritual body' that we shall receive in the age to come. Berkhof points out that this expression should not be interpreted as meaning 'a body made out of uncorporeal material (whatever that may be)'. What Paul means is *a soma*, a total human existence, soul and body included, which will be created, permeated, and controlled by the Spirit of Christ.'[39]

Today, however, we still find ourselves in the *interim*, which is characterized by two terms: 'already' and 'not yet'. *Not yet* for the Kingdom in its fullness and perfection is still to come. But also: *already*, for Jesus Christ has reconciled us to God and has given us his Spirit as the foretaste of the coming Kingdom. It is my firm conviction that in the Christian Church we generally give far too little attention and weight to this 'already'. To put it in a Pauline perspective, we are more convinced of the truth of Romans 7, the chapter that deals with the internal struggle in the Christian, than of that of Romans 8, the chapter that speaks of the life in the Spirit. And I am afraid that this is largely due to *our preaching* and *our theology*. We should

38. J. B. Lightfoot, *Notes on Epistles of St Paul from unpublished commentaries* (1895), p. 324.
39. Berkhof, *op.cit.*, p. 108.

seriously ask ourselves whether the lack of certainty about the presence of the Holy Spirit, which unfortunately is characteristic of so many church people, is not due to a similar lack in our preaching and theology. Yes, let us take one more step and ask ourselves: Is it perhaps due to our *own* lack of experience of the presence of the spirit? Over a hundred and fifty years ago Charles Simeon pointed out that technical theologians often have a certain uneasiness in dealing with the work of the Spirit, because the Spirit's ministry is so closely involved in the vital issues of Christian living and thinking, that the theologian must be carefully tuned in on his own sanctification in order to deal with it adequately.[40]

In addition, many ministers and theologians are afraid of putting much emphasis on experience, because they are scared of *excesses and divisions* in the congregation and the church at large. It must be admitted that things can easily go wrong. We see this in the congregation at Corinth, which clearly was an experience-oriented congregation. Bruner mentions three serious mistakes the Corinthian charismatics made: they were always out for *more*, for *power* and for *evidence*.[41] Over against these three errors Paul puts three *sola's: solus Christus, sola gratia* and *sola fides*. At the same time, however, we should carefully notice that Paul does not oppose *too much* attention to the Spirit and experience by *less* attention, but by *proper* attention! Paul would like them all to live by the spirit. He longs for a Spirit-filled congregation, that is, a congregation with real experience of the Spirit. But this is possible only when they pass the three tests mentioned before. (1) It must be a congregation that confesses Jesus as Lord and finds its basis and centre in him. (2) It must be a congregation that is the body of Christ, so that all members, with their gifts, function in such a way that they support and build each other up. (3) It must be a congre-

40. *Cf.* Lovelace, *op.cit.*, p. 122.
41. Bruner, *op.cit.*, pp. 307ff.

gation that is mission-minded and uses its gifts to draw others to Christ. I believe these tests also apply to all claims of personal experience. And if some claims or some experiences cannot pass these tests, let us then remember that a wrong emphasis on experience can never be righted by the denial or oppression of experience, but only by correcting it and redirecting it towards Scripturally controlled experience.